32 programs to help kids know Jesus

JAFFA 1
32 programs to help kids know Jesus

Scripture Union
Resources for Ministry Unit
Locked Bag 2
Central Coast Business Centre
NSW 2252 Australia

Distributed in the UK by
Scripture Union
207-209 Queensway
Bletchley
Milton Keynes MK2 2EB

Jesus a friend for all: 32 programs to help kids know Jesus.

Includes index.

ISBN 1 876794 09 7.

1. Bible - Study and teaching (Primary) - Activity programs.
2. Jesus Christ - Study and teaching (Primary) - Activity programs.
3. Christianity - Study and teaching (Primary) - Activity programs.
4. Christian life - Study and teaching (Primary) - Activity programs.
I. Scripture Union Australia.

      268.432

This resource has been commissioned, written, steered and edited by the members of the National Primary Schools Network, Australia and New Zealand
> Brent Allred
> Anita Bowyer
> Jenny Lanyon
> Helen Phillips
> Glen Simpkins
> Sally Smith
> Terry Williams

Additional writers
> Jenny Begg
> Kathryn Churchett
> Leanne Palmer
> Lesley Vince
> Shauna Woods

Editor
> Sally Smith

Graphics and Layout
> Ivan Smith

Contents

A Great Start

The Big G

The BOOK

Reality Check!

Setting the pace

Issues

What's a SUPA kids club?

Throughout the world, every week kids of varying ages meet with leaders to encounter Jesus through the Bible and through relationship with each other. In clubs like these, many of the kids have no contact with churches and their club is the only regular opportunity they have to explore the Christian faith.

In Australia many primary schools have SUPA clubs (Scripture Union Primary Clubs), which exist to introduce young people to Jesus, the Bible and the local church. In these clubs leaders and kids learn about Jesus together through the Bible, prayer and relationships.

If you run a SUPA Club or another kids club with the same aims, JAFFA is for you. The programs are written by experienced children's ministry coordinators who know and love primary aged kids and work closely with kid's club leaders.

This book is part of a 3 volume series, JAFFA 1,2 and 3, which form a three year syllabus. Each volume contains 32 programs to cover a year, leaving some spare weeks for seasonal or special programs.

Each program has 3 sections (which can be 5 or 10 minutes in length) and a snappy finish. There are plenty of activities included for groups with more time.

Section 1: **Open the pack** – Physical activities to introduce the theme and involve everyone and so create an atmosphere that communicates, 'It's great to be here!'

Section 2: **Dig in** – Interacting with the truth from the Bible in a way that pushes thinking and encourages exploration.

Section 3: **Chew on it** – Involves thinking about how the Bible truth applies to us and encourages some sort of a response

Because it's impossible to develop a top program with these elements that caters effectively for ages 5-12, each section usually has two suggested activities

  one for the 9-11 year old age group

  the other either for 5-8 year olds

  or mixed ages.

This will allow you to choose activities to suit your group.

We hope you have fun with JAFFA 1 and that through it, you and your group get to know Jesus better.

Best practice in Children's ministry

So you're running an effective kids club?
That's great!

You've built up a good rapport with your group and feel you're really getting somewhere. The kids are exploring the Bible and finding out about Jesus for themselves. They're asking questions and telling others what a good time they have each week.

But important as your relationship is with the kids in your club, there are other important relationships to consider as well.

FAMILY Each child is part of a family and you need to consider that family in what you do. Take every opportunity to be inclusive of other family members. Even though they sometimes act as though they are independent, primary school children are still influenced greatly by their parents. There are ideas for organizing a family event on page 8.

SCHOOL If yours is a school club, you and the club have to fit comfortably with the school. It's worth putting in the effort to get to know the office staff and teachers. Keep them informed about what you are doing, even if they don't seem very interested.

CHURCH No matter how good your program is, it will be better with the support and involvement of other Christians. The church is God's plan for people to be nurtured in the faith, however, unfortunately not all churches are child-friendly. You may need to be an advocate, approaching local churches to ask what they can do to include kids from your club. Don't think it's too hard. Churches who are prepared to rethink their agendas for those outside, usually benefit as much as those they seek to include. Other churches may already have a good church kids program but not realise that you would like to link your kids into it. If you are a school parachurch group, meet with your local ministers and explain what you are trying to do for the kids in your area. Ask for their support. It takes extra effort, but it's worth it.

We suggest you run one activity a term to help your group make these connections with Family, Church and School. You can start with these:

- A SUPA JAFFA DO to run for your school (Page 6)
- A family bush BBQ (Page 8)
- A church visit and debrief (Page 10)

important relationships....

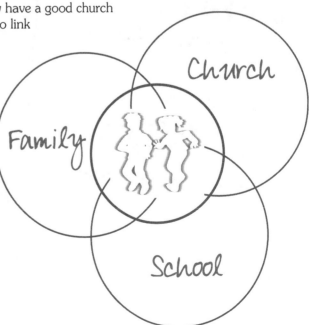

Church

Family

School

JAFFA DO

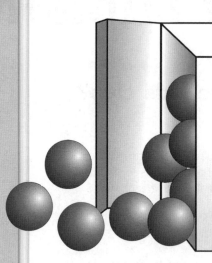

In Australia kids love to munch bright orange covered small chocolate balls called Jaffas. If you're not lucky enough to be able to buy them where you live, you can use other round sweets instead.

SUPA Clubs are encouraged to put on a SUPA DO for their school once in a while. It's a chance to give the whole school a fun time and let everyone know about SUPA Club. It can be adapted for a church to put on for a kids club or vice versa.

Below is a 'smorgasbord' of ideas. Choose those that are most suited to your space and time constraints - and naturally the ones you think will be the most fun.

Here come some SUPA JAFFA DO activities for you to choose from:

JAFFA and Spoon Race

YOU WILL NEED

- Jaffas and a spoon for each child

Substitute Jaffas for eggs and you already know how to play this one.

JAFFA Chase

YOU WILL NEED

- Lots of Jaffas • A plastic garbage bag
- Level playground area •

Choose ten children to line up side by side and give each a Jaffa. The aim is for them to roll their Jaffa along the ground to the finish line. If lots of children would like to be involved you may want to have a couple of heats (probably no more than five or the spectators may get a little restless). After you have run all your heats, bring the winner from each heat back to try out for the JAFFA Chase Championship. Run the final with the winner being crowned JAFFA Chase Champion (a gold cardboard crown with those words on it would add to the effect).

JAFFA Roundabout

YOU WILL NEED

- Teams of eight and you've guessed it ... •

Seat the teams in circles. Give each a Jaffa to roll along the ground behind their backs around the circle until it gets back to the one who started. They yell 'Jaffa!' and send the Jaffa round again, then they are given another, so two are going round together. As each comes back to the beginning they yell 'Jaffa!' again and add a third and fourth Jaffa. The winning team is the one who completes the fourth circuit with all four Jaffas.

JAFFA face painting

YOU WILL NEED

- Youknowwhats (the round orange ones), buckets of water, face wipes •

Wet fingers and Jaffas produce orange paint. And once the orange comes off there's another colour to work with. Challenge teams to decorate each others faces in brown and orange with a prize for the best team.

Over to you ...

What other games can you adapt to suit your JAFFA DO?

Finish with a short and snappy explanation of what your SUPA club or JAFFA group is about and an invitation for children of the appropriate age to come.

For a SUPA club it could go something like this:

'Today we've enjoyed lots of SUPA JAFFA activities. (Hold up signs 'SUPA' and 'JAFFA') SUPA stands for Scripture Union Primary Age and these have been SUPA Activities because they have been organised for you to enjoy by the SUPA Club here at your school. SUPA Club is for children in Years......(depending on your club) and happens at this time every week in.......(name the room).

In SUPA Club we find out about someone absolutely super. Not Superman but someone super terrific. Not someone with lots of money; not a president or a politician but someone who makes a huge change to the way we live. This super terrific person changed the world and changed people's lives nearly 2000 years ago. This person is still changing people's lives today. In fact he has changed my life. If you'd like to find out more about someone who's super-terrific, why not come along to SUPA Club next week and discover more about him with us?'

A Family

A program to involve families

Decorations: Put real or fake branches of gum trees above doorways and around the walls if you have to be inside, but hopefully you can enjoy lots of sunshine (and flies(?) outdoors). Collect as many toy koalas as possible and put them in the branches. If you can tether a sheep or two nearby all the better.

Fancy Dress: Shorts and T-shirts with thongs are perfect. And why not sew a few dangling corks onto a hat?

Food: Dry biscuits with vegemite, sausages in bread (with tomato sauce of course) and lamingtons for that finishing touch.
A table with cut damper, a tub of margarine, a tin of golden syrup and plastic knives can be on hand for would-be snackers to help themselves.

Background Music: Anything from **Slim Dusty** to **John Williamson** and **Colin Buchanan**.

If you can get along an Aussie bush band all the better. Failing that these tracks from *Gospelling to the Beat 1* (Available from Scripture Union and Christian bookshops) have an Aussie flavour: *Holy Gospel, G'day, g'day!*
Greatest man

Games: Encourage everyone to 'have a go'. Winning isn't important but having fun is. In keeping with the Aussie tradition of backyard cricket, have a bat and ball and a couple a garbage bins in place for an impromptu game. A volleyball net strung between two trees and a ball might encourage some to have fun imitating the 2000 Games beach volleyball win.
Informality is the order of the day.

Suggested program

Welcome and thanks for coming

Song – G'day, g'day! If you're really adventurous try it as a round as well.

Gumboot throwing competition – Give everyone a go at standing behind a line and heaving the boot as far as possible towards a target.

A bit about the club – (from a leader)

Newspaper dress up – Divide into groups with families together. Provide lots of newspaper and a roll of masking tape for each group and let them dress an adult as the Man from Snowy River complete with hat and long coat.

What we do at club – (from the children) Give the kids 5 minutes max to sing, show and say what they like best. Make sure it's fun, visual and that everyone can hear.

Bush BBQ

Sing off – Give groups paper and pencil and 5 minutes to make up a song about Australia to the tune of Waltzing Matilda. Let them perform it for everyone with lagerphone accompaniment.

Think Spot – Tell the story of Granny Smith and affirm your belief that God can make something significant and useful out of what others overlook.

The story of Granny Smith

In the early days of Australia, there was a pioneer woman called Maria Anne Smith who lived on a farm in what is now the Sydney suburb of Eastwood. She was the town midwife and because she had delivered so many of the children in the area and was well loved in the community she was called Granny Smith.

One day she bought a barrel of crabapples to make apple tarts. Half the barrel was rotten and unusable so she emptied them on the compost heap. Some months later she saw a tree growing up from the rotten apples. She dug it up and transplanted it away from the rubbish and later it produced green apples that were good for eating. The apples became very popular in the area, where people called them Granny Smith's apples. They were the first green eating apples in Australia and now they are know even overseas.

'How did you grow these apples?' people would ask Granny Smith.

She couldn't really explain it but she would think of the tree that grew up from the rotten apples and tell them,

'Isn't it just like God – the very stuff we chuck away, God uses to bring in a new thing.'

Recipe for damper

Sift 3 cups of plain flour, 1 tsp of salt, 2 tsps cream of tartar, 1 tsp bicarb soda into a bowl. Mix well with a fork and add tepid water to make a stiff dough. Knead on a floured board for 1 minute then form into a round about 50mm high. Place on foil in a very hot oven for 40 minutes or until it sounds hollow when tapped.

How to make a lagerphone

- Grab a broom handle, hammer, 20 flat headed nails (about 3cm long) and as many metal bottle caps.

- Hammer the bottle caps onto the broom handle randomly, leaving them loose enough to rattle. Leave a space all around the middle to hold it.

- Play it by thumping it up and down on the floor in time to the music.

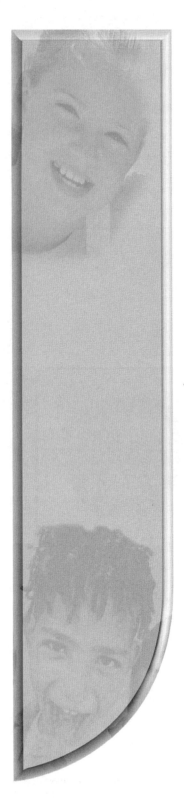

Being part of a church is God's plan for his people so no matter how difficult it is, kids' club leaders needs to try hard to link their children into a local church. If yours is a school group with children from several local churches, do your best to involve all those churches in your club in as many ways as possible. If your group is already attached to a church the link may be more natural, but it still needs to be worked at. Start with letting the church(es) know about the group. Here are just a few suggestions

- Arrange to visit a church service, home group or other church activity to share about your kids' club and your goals

- Deliver to the church(es) an attractive poster with photos taken at some of your activities twice a year and enlist their prayer support

- Send out a club prayer update to keep the church(es) informed.
  (Make sure the school also receives a copy if yours is a school club.)

- Invite suitable, interested people from the church(es) to help in your group. They may be able to prepare craft materials, play a guitar for the singing or give an interesting talk either as a one off or regularly. Make sure that all visitors to a school group comply with the school's guidelines.

Church Excursion!

Keeping local churches informed is one side of making church links. The other is to give the children an experience of being part of the church. One way is to have a group 'excursion' to a church worship service. It will take some planning to get parental permission and work out how to get the children there, but if well done, it's worth it.

No matter how much you enjoy taking risks, don't just arrive with the children. Plan ahead.

Group and Church

Here are some steps to make the most of the visit:

1. **Talk to the minister and other key people several weeks beforehand, letting them know what you hope to accomplish by the visit.** The service shouldn't revolve around the children, nor should they be asked to 'perform'. You want them to experience the church at worship. Some parts of the service may require a short explanation for the children and other visitors and this should be done naturally without interrupting the flow of the service.

2. **Arrange for several people to speak informally to the children as soon as they arrive to make them feel welcome.**

3. **Make sure the children know what to expect.** The week before, it would be helpful to run through what might happen, how long it is likely to take and what is expected of them at each point, allowing them to ask questions.

4. **Think about whether it would be useful to provide a pencil and 'Here's what happened' card for each child to fill in.** In some cases it could distract, but in others it will help keep them quiet and focused.

5. **After the service a 'debrief' will help the children process what they have seen, heard and done.** A few church members might like to serve morning tea and be part of a discussion with your group. These questions could be asked of the children by the church members. The children might like to ask the church members the same questions.

    - What did you enjoy most today?
    - What did you find strange?
    - Did anything surprise you?
    - Is there anything you'd like to know?
    - Has today changed the way you think of God, the church, people who go to church?

> Photocopiable sheet for the kids to record their observations.

Here's what happened in **church**

(Write or draw what you notice.)

Before it started

I heard …. _____

I noticed … _____

It started with …

_____

How many people had something to say from the front? *(Cross the number as each new person speaks)*

1 2 3 4 5 6 7 8 9 10 11 12

What's something unusual about church?

_____

Was a musical instrument played?   YES   NO

Did everyone sing together?   YES   NO
How many times?   1   2   3   4   5   6   7   8   9   10

How many times was the Bible read?
1   2   3   4   5   6   7   8   9   10

Were other books used?   YES   NO

Was there something special for children?   YES   NO

Was there something special for old people?   YES   NO

What did people do?
SING   PRAY   READ   DANCE   THINK   LAUGH
TALK   SHAKE   HANDS   KNEEL

What was the main talk about?

_____

What was the last thing that happened?

_____

Why do you think people go to church?

_____

1 ☼ff to a great start

For the leader

Read Mark 10:13-16 and Psalm 139:13-16 and think about what they mean for you and the children in your group.

All children are precious to God who knows and loves each one. This club provides an excellent opportunity to let children know they are welcome, especially children who may not feel that way elsewhere. Spend some time now praying that God will help you to make the most of this opportunity, that you will be like Jesus to all the children and that through you they will see something of God.

When the club is starting out everyone is keyed on you and you are setting the tone for participation. Enthusiastically join in doing the things you are asking the children to do and encourage all helpers and children to do the same, whether it's playing a game or sharing an opinion. Every child should feel included, valued and safe in the club environment.

 If your group has never used Bibles before you may prefer to read the story dramatically or have the verses written on a large sheet of paper or overhead projector sheets. But always show them the Bible where the verses come from so they become familiar with it.

Before the session mark the place in the children's Bibles with a bookmark to make it easier for them to find.

· ·

☼pen the pack

Why? To create a fun atmosphere and get to know each other

Needed: Balloons, poster with club name or logo, four large cards.
On one side write the numbers 1-4. (SUPA clubs can write the letters S,U,P,A instead.) On the other side write 'Games', 'Music', 'Jesus', '?'.

Have some bright music playing. Cover the floor with balloons. Rub others on your sleeve so the static electricity lets them stick to the ceiling. As the children enter the room allow them to kick and throw the balloons while moving around to the music. Then tell them to burst all the balloons (including the ones on the ceiling).

Direct everyone to sit down in front of a poster containing your club name or logo. Welcome them to the club and introduce yourself if necessary.

Display the numbered side of the four cards. Turn each card over and as you do talk briefly about each element and answer questions.

- **Games** ... all sorts of games will be played.
  (You might like to invite children to say their favourites.)
- **Music** ... there'll be songs or music.
  (You could show the covers of some cassettes or CD you plan to use.)
- **Jesus** ... every week we will hear about Jesus, read about Jesus, ask questions about Jesus, talk to Jesus.
- **?** ... and every so often there will be a surprise or two.

SAY G'DAY

Needed: A copy of Appendix 1 Say G'Day for everyone, pencils.
Some sweets for leaders to give out when someone says 'Hi!' to them.

Get everybody to move around the group and collect a different signature for each box on their page.

Sidebar

Main idea

You are welcome here and you matter to God.

Questions answered

by this program

- What is this group?
- Can I join?
- What's going to happen here?

Bible Base

Matthew 19:13-14

SONG: G'DAY, G'DAY

Needed: *Gospelling to the Beat 2 CD and player or leader with an instrument.*

Play *G'day, g'day.* Set an appropriate challenge, for the group to try to complete before the song finishes. It may be to give everyone a high five one or more times or handshake 15 different people.

Comment: Everyone here is welcome and part of our club. Jesus came because people, all people, matter to God.

Dig in

JESUS AND CHILDREN

Why? To find out from the Bible how Jesus treated children.

> ***Pose the questions:*** What does Jesus think of children? How can we be sure?

Invite responses and explain that we can't ask Jesus now because he returned to heaven nearly 2000 years ago but we can read in the Bible the way he treated children.

Distribute the Bibles and direct children to Matthew 19.

Explain that a man who knew Jesus very well wrote this part of the Bible. Matthew saw this happen.

Ask for a volunteer to read verses 13 and 14.

> ***Pose the question:*** What does this tell us about how Jesus treated children?

Chew on it

Why? To encourage them to think about themselves in relation to Jesus.

Invite everyone to imagine how they would feel if they were one of those children. How would they feel when the disciples wanted to send them away? What about when Jesus said to let them come? Have everyone think of one word to describe their feelings.

PRAYERS

If you think it's appropriate you might show how to turn their word into a prayer such as 'Jesus, I'm glad you like children. It makes me feel special. Thanks!' Suggest that those who want pray, substituting their own word for 'special'.

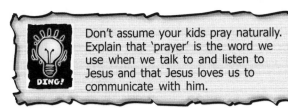
Don't assume your kids pray naturally. Explain that 'prayer' is the word we use when we talk to and listen to Jesus and that Jesus loves us to communicate with him.

MEETING JESUS

Form groups of 4-5 children to make up a role play of the Bible passage to show everyone.

Close the pack

Comment: Children are very special to Jesus. Every person is very special to him. At this club we'll get to know Jesus as well as each other.

Off to a great start

Main idea

I matter to God; therefore I need to treat other people remembering that they matter to God too.

Questions answered

by this program

- What am I allowed to do in this group?
- What am I not allowed to do?
- How can I help to make this club the best place to be?

Bible Base

Matthew
22:36-39

For the leader

Children operate within sets of boundaries wherever they are - at home, at school, in the street. These boundaries help them to grow towards self-discipline. Your club will need to have a set of boundaries to encourage children to operate as a group and enjoy their times together. School based clubs need to reinforce the general rules of the school. Other clubs need to develop their own. When children are involved setting rules they are far more likely to keep them. Your role as leader then, is to point out the choices they have when a rule has been broken and encourage good choices.

Prepare beforehand 12 pieces of A4 paper each with a letter from the word 'CONSEQUENCES' written on one side. On the reverse side, in order, number the pieces. Fold each piece 4-6 times. As children arrive, give out the pieces, asking them to put it in their pocket for later.

· ·

 Open the pack

Why? To think about the importance of rules.

LINE JAZZ

Form teams of 4-10, lined up behind their leader. Explain that teams will gain points for being the first to rearrange themselves and sit down in the order you announce. Play several heats using these orders.

(Don't forget to check that the order is correct!)

1. Tallest to shortest

2. Alphabetical order on your first name

3. Youngest to oldest

4. Lightest to darkest skin colour

5. Shortest to tallest

The important part of this game is in the scoring. Be completely arbitrary in allocating points. For example, in the first heat, the winning team gains 50 bonus points because the person at the front of the line has blue eyes. In the second heat the slowest team gets 200 bonus points because someone had corn flakes for breakfast. Very soon the teams will begin to get confused and possibly upset because this is 'unfair'. Don't pursue the game too long.

Pose the question: What would make this game better?

YOU SET THE RULES

Form four groups. Ask each to decide on the most important two rules for the following situations, a different situation for each group.

1. Stranded on a desert island.	2. In a football crowd.
3. In charge of the class.	4. Sleep over at your house.

Let groups share their rules.

Dig in

JESUS RULES

Why? To find out what Jesus said were the two most important rules.

Needed: Bibles or a bright poster with the words of Matthew 22:36-39.

Explain that Jesus told people God's rules. Read the words together.

SHOW ME!

Why? To think through the meaning of loving God and loving others

Give pairs or groups two minutes to think of a way of expressing Jesus' two most important rules in sign language.

 # Chew on it

Pose the question: How could we make sure we kept those two rules in our club?

Discuss specific ways of showing love for others. Write up rules you agree would make the club enjoyable and safe for everyone. You might like to use this acronym.

R espect everyone
U se only good words
L isten when others are speaking
E njoy yourself and help others to enjoy themselves too
S it, unless invited to move

Invite the children who received letters to arrange themselves in order of the numbers to reveal the word 'CONSEQUENCES'.

Next to each line, discuss what the fair consequences might be if someone chooses not to keep that rule. For example if someone speaks or acts disrespectfully they need to apologise and try not to do it again.

GOD HELPS US KEEP THE RULES

Why? As a reminder that God will help us do what he wants and to start the children praying aloud in the group.

Invite someone to pray that you will all love God and love others better through the club.

 If children are not comfortable with praying, pray a sentence prayer yourself. Suggest someone write one at home and bring it to pray in the group next time.

LINE JAZZ AGAIN

Why? To show that groups work much better when everyone knows the rules

Finish with some different heats of Line Jazz, but this time with fair scoring.

 # Close the pack

Explain that you'll write up the rules and bring them each week.

We need to love God and love others and our club rules will help us do that.

3

Main idea

God created the world and everything in it.

Questions answered

by this program

- How do we know there is a God?
- Who is God?
- Who made God?
- What is God like?
- What does God do?
- How and why did God create?

Bible Base

Gen 1;
Psalm 24:1-2;
Psalm 33:6-9;
Jeremiah 32:17

God - Creator

For the leader

The Bible begins with God (Genesis 1:1). No one created God; he has always existed. If any other being or power had created God then *they* would be God. The Bible tells us that God created all things. He spoke and they came into being. The existence of ourselves and the world around us is a good reason for some to believe in a creator but many children are happy to believe that the world just happened. It's better to let the Bible speak for itself than to try and argue the point.

Although we cannot see God and certainly will never fully understand him, we can discover some things about him from what he has made. The immensity of our universe and the infinite detail of the microscopic world speak of God's greatness, intelligence, creativity and power. We know that God is also personal, just as we are who are created in God's image.

God planned to create the world and pronounced the finished creation 'very good' (Gen. 1:31).

The Bible reminds us that this is God's world, not ours and we need to live in it responsibly. Everything in it belongs to God, including us. God deserves our love and gratitude and worship for all he has given us. Ultimately all of creation from the beginning of time until the end is under God's control.

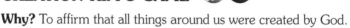

 Open the pack

CREATION KIM'S GAME

Why? To affirm that all things around us were created by God.

Needed: Up to twenty objects on a tray, covered with a cloth. Include some natural objects like stones, flowers and shells.

Either give each player a pencil or paper or have a blackboard or overhead projector available. Gather everyone around the tray. Remove the cloth for thirty seconds and then replace it. Let everyone either write down individually, or tell you to write down, everything on the tray that God has made. When all the natural objects are named, recall some of the others and see who can track them back through the manufacturing process to what God made. For example, a book is made from paper, which comes from trees.

WHO MADE IT?

Why? To get the group questioning about where the world came from.

Needed: A selection of articles that have labels on them indicating where they were made, for example a stuffed toy, shirt, watch and plate.

Select some children to try and discover where each was made.

Comment: Sometimes it's easy to find out where something was made. My big question is 'Who made the world?'

Accept the children's answers, encouraging honest statement of their beliefs and why they believe that way, even if they are not biblical. You should also state your belief and say why in one sentence.

 # Dig in

WHAT IT SAYS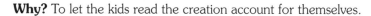

Why? To let the kids read the creation account for themselves.

Form small groups each with a CEV Bible. Allow 5 minutes for groups to read Genesis 1 and agree on what they think is the most interesting thing in it. Share findings.

LET'S START AT THE BEGINNING

Why? To hear the creation account and think about it.

Needed: A bell or horn

Start reading at Genesis 1:1 and explain that whenever they hear something about the creation of the world they have to run to the centre and use the bell or horn. The first to sound it has to say what they heard about creation.

 # Chew on it

QUESTION BOX

Why? To evoke wonder at God's creation.

Comment that there are things you don't understand about the creation, such as 'How do spiders know how to make a web?' and 'How do migrating birds find their way?' Have a leader write down questions as the children think of them. Issue a challenge to discover the answer to any of these questions before next session.

TWO WORLDS

Why? To get beyond the question of whether or not God created and think about what it might mean if he did.

Needed: Enlarged copy of Appendix 2 The people of Ig and Og, *cut in half*

Display Appendix 2. Explain that they are two imaginary worlds. The people on Og are sure their world came about from dust particles flying through space and everything in their world including themselves has no reason for existing. The people on Ig are sure God made them and their world and that God is still interested in them.

> **Pose the questions:** *Which world would you like to belong to and why?*

How does that relate to us?

 # Close the pack

The Bible says that God created this world and everything in it, including us.

ACTIVE PRAYER

Have everyone think of one created thing to thank God for. Form a line or a circle. Start out with everyone saying together 'Thanks God for ....' then go along the line or around the circle Mexican wave style as people add their word. After the last person all say 'Amen' together.

4 God - Rule Maker

Main idea

God gave
the Ten
Commandments
so his people
would know how
they should live
as his people.

Questions
answered

by this program

- How do I know what is right and what is wrong?
- Do we have to obey the 10 commandments to get to heaven ?
- Why did God give us rules to live by?

Bible Base

Exodus 19,
20:1-20;
Matt 5-7;
John 14:15,
23-24;
John 15:7-17.

For the leader

When God miraculously saved the Israelites by freeing them from slavery in Egypt they knew that they were God's people. Three months after their 'salvation' when God gave them the Ten Commandments and other laws, they knew what God expected of them as his people. Obedience didn't make them God's people. They were already his. Keeping the law was their right response to a God who was committed to them. Keeping the Commandments doesn't save us but doing what God wants marks us out as his people.

The first four commandments cover the basics of the divine- human relationship and the last six commandments cover the basics of the human- human relationships.

. . . .

 Open the pack

BUS BITS GAME

Why? The parts of a vehicle do what they are designed for and that makes the bus do what it is designed for. God's people keep God's rules to be the people of God.

Divide into groups of 4 to 10. (Two or three teams is best.) Give each member of the team the name of a part of a bus such as steering wheel, window or accelerator. The team leader is the driver. Each team has the same names and numbers of parts and a driver. The teams are seated in rows behind their leaders and level with their corresponding parts from the other teams. Try to match children of equal ability. The leader tells a story about a bus and as each part is mentioned the team members with that name have to run up to the front and right down to the back around chairs and back to their place. The winner scores a point for their team. When the leader mentions the word 'bus' the whole team has to stay in order and run around the chairs and back to their places. For safety, set out the rules clearly before you start.

DISCUSSION

Pose the questions:

How can people know which school you go to?

How can people know someone is in the police force?

How can people tell if you like (a certain pop group)?

How can people tell who are people who believe in God?

Explain that God wanted his people to be different from the other nations so he gave them rules to live by. When they kept these people would know that they were God's people.

 # Dig in

VIDEO CLIP

Why? To familiarize the group with the Ten Commandments and the account of how they were given.

Show a video clip from *Prince of Egypt* where Moses goes up Mt Sinai and is given the Ten Commandments.

THE 10 COMMANDMENTS

Display 10 numbered sheets with these references around the room.

1.Exodus 20:2	2.Exodus 20:3	3.Exodus 20:4	4.Exodus 20:7
5.Exodus 20:8	6.Exodus 20:12	7.Exodus 20:13	8.Exodus 20:14
9.Exodus 20:15	10.Exodus 20:16		

Distribute Bibles and let pairs of children choose a sheet, find and read the verse and write it on the reverse side of the sheet.

 # Chew on it

RULES FOR US

Needed: 10 blown up balloons each with one of these summary statements written on a piece of paper inside. Bibles with Exodus 20:1-20 marked.

Pose the question: *What do the 10 Commandments mean for us today?*

Select children, one at a time, to burst a balloon to find the short summary inside, then with the help of the group find the matching commandment.

Summary Statements:

1. God is always number one	2. God is the greatest
3. God's name is special	4. God invented holidays
5. Parents rule. OK!	6. Take care of each other.
7. Let's be faithful	8. Give and don't take
9. Truth is best	10. Enjoy what you've got.

HOW TO LIVE

Needed: *10 balloons containing summary statements as above.*

Break the balloons together. (You may need the help of a pin.) Collect the summary statements and attach them to a board. Read them with the explanation that this is how God asked his people to live to show that he was important to them.

Pose the question: *How can we show people that God is important to us?*

 # Close the pack

People who are serious about following God's way will live the way he wants. When they do, people will know they are different.

God – the very

Main idea

God is like a loving father to all who turn from their own way and come back to him.

Questions answered

by this program

- How is God like our Father?
- If God is our Father why do bad things still happen to us?
- How can I belong to God's family?

Bible Base

Luke 15:11-32

For the leader

The image of God as our father is wonderfully meaningful to some Christians expressing love, comfort, provision and safety. For others, the father image has negative connotations evoking memories of neglect, disappointment or abuse.

But God is portrayed in the Bible as the Father of his people and most children have some idea of what the very best father might be like. We need to help children to discover that their Father God loves them unconditionally and that they can trust and love him. We can help them to find out the ways that God shows his love to them and help them see that their Father God is the greatest Dad- better even than their idea of a perfect Dad. We must also be sensitive to the fact that many children are part of single parent families (usually living with their mother) or blended/stepfamilies and some children are victims of their father's abuse. These factors affect a child's perception of what a 'father' is

God is the Father of everyone only in so far as he is our creator. Everyone is not born naturally into God's family but we become God's children as we put our faith in Jesus and he adopts us into his family. (John 1:12)

· ·

 Open the pack

CHOCOLATE DAD

Why? To have fun and introduce the theme of fathers.

Needed: knife, fork, block of chocolate on a plate, die, hat coat and tie.

Seat the group in a circle with everything in the centre. Take turns to throw the die. When someone throws a six they move to the centre, put on the hat, coat and tie and once 'dressed' begin eating the chocolate with the knife and fork (one piece at a time). The die continues around the circle until someone else throws a six, then that person takes over.

FATHER ACROSTIC

Write FATHER vertically down the board. Ask the group for words or phrases beginning with each letter to describe the characteristics of a father.

- Faithful, forgiving, fun, feeds me
- Awesome, affectionate, away a lot
- Teaches me things, too hard
- Helps, hears,
- Encourages, exciting
- Remembers birthdays, reliable

Comment: 'I don't know about your dad, but I do know that some kids have good dads, some haven't got a dad because he's died or left and some even have two dads. But I think we all have some idea of what the best dad would be like. God is like the very best dad you can imagine.'

Explain that the Bible says a lot about God being like a father.

best Father

 ## Dig in

THE LOVING FATHER

Using your best storytelling manner, read the story from Luke 15:11-24 in the CEV or have some older children read it to the group.

 ## Chew on it

WHAT DOES IT MEAN?

Needed: *Two sheet of paper, one with the heading 'FATHER' on one side and 'GOD' on the reverse and the other with 'SON' on one side and 'ME' on the reverse. Copies of Appendix 3, How to turn to God*

Display the two sheets labelled 'FATHER' and 'SON'. Ask the children to suggest words that describe the father and the son in the story. List them.

Turn over both sheets.

Comment: People sometimes go away from God like the son left his father.

APPENDIX 3

Form groups of 3-5 and give each a copy of Appendix 3 to find out how a person can come back to God.

APPENDIX 3

Use an enlarged copy of Appendix 3 and explain that some of the children in the picture have gone away from God. They've not bothered about him. They've done what they like. When they realise their mistake and are sorry and want to be friends with God again, they can pray a Thank you-Sorry-Please prayer like the one on the sheet.

 ## Close the pack

WHAT ABOUT US?

Pose the question:
How can we come back to God and be part of his family when
we know we've gone away from him?

Encourage the children to tell you based on what they discovered from the sheet.

If you did the father acrostic circle the words that apply to God.

PRAYER

Invite someone to read this prayer for the group

Thank you God for being the very best father there is.
Please help us to be children that you're proud of.

God ~ Freedom

For the leader

This world has been messed up by people choosing not to live God's way.

However God still loves us and has promised to be always with us, giving strength and courage to face life with its struggles. God's plan for our lives is good and those things that are hard and painful, God can use ultimately for our good (Romans 8:28). As well, God has also provided the means for us to enter into an eternal life with him, overflowing with blessings and free from the limitations of this life. It's our choice whether or not we accept it.

Christians are not exempt from the consequences of evil and death in this world, but from an eternal perspective, we are safe with God in heaven forever.

 Don't try to do too much. For a 20-30 minute program choose just one activity from each section.

. . . .

 ☼ Open the box

WHO'S THE LEADER?

Why? To get the idea of a hidden 'someone' being behind what happens in the world but it only becomes obvious who it is as everyone follows him.

One child is chosen to leave the room while the rest sit in a circle. A 'leader' is then chosen who begins doing an action such as clapping, clicking fingers or scratching knees and everyone else copies. The absent child returns and tries to guess who is the 'leader'. The 'leader' needs to keep changing the action every 15 seconds until he/she is discovered. The 'leader' then leaves the room and a new 'leader' is chosen.

PUPPETS

Needed: A simple marionette puppet. You can make one from a rag doll, string and two rulers.

Explain that God made people but he doesn't make us do what he says. (Not like they followed the leader in the game or like a puppeteer controls a puppet.) If you have a string puppet, make it do some tricks and then cut the strings to show that God doesn't control what we do. When God created the first people, Adam and Eve, he gave them the freedom to choose.

 Dig in

WHAT HAPPENED TO GOD'S PERFECT WORLD?

Why? To learn about when the first people chose to disobey God.

Needed: *A chart with these questions and references:*

1. What was God's rule? What choice did the man have? Genesis 2:15-17
2. What did the man and woman decide? Genesis 3:1-8
3. What were the consequences? Genesis 3:13-24

Display the chart then distribute Bibles and help the children to look up and read the passages to discover the answers.

Giver

THUMBS UP, THUMBS DOWN

Why? To actively listen to the Bible account of Adam and Eve choosing to disobey God.

Comment: We all make choices and those choices have consequences. The first people had to choose whether or not to do what God said. The Bible tells what happened.

Ask the children to listen as you read and when they hear something bad (like 'you will die before the day is over') do 'thumbs down'. When they hear something good (like 'God said we could eat fruit from any tree in the garden') do 'thumbs up'.

Read Genesis 2:15-17 then Genesis 3:1-13.

As a break from reading, ask if anyone knows what happened next. Be enthusiastic about being able to check what they might have heard against the original Bible story. Encourage the thumbs up, thumbs down again as you read Genesis 3:14-24.

Chew on it

WHAT DOES IT MEAN?

Why? To understand that our choices contribute to the imperfect world.

Comment: Even though the first people made a poor choice, God keeps on giving us the freedom to make choices today. We don't have to live God's way, but we do have to live with the consequences of what we do.

Show pictures of war, homelessness, poverty, etc.

> ***Pose the question:***
> *How does that story from the Bible help us to understand why these things happen today?* (People's selfishness or greed causes problems for others.)

DISCUSSION

Why? To help process the story and what it means.

Make a group 'snake' by making a line and having everyone put their hands on the shoulders of the person in front of them. 'Hiss' around for a bit and then sit down. Retell the story by asking questions like: What was God's rule? What did the snake say about the rule? Who did the people obey, God or the snake? What did God say was going to happen because they didn't obey him? Why couldn't the people be close to God after that.

> ***Pose the question:***
> *What happens when we don't keep God's rules?*
> (It leads to us and other people being unhappy. It stops us being close to God.)

Close the pack

God doesn't make us do what he says, but when we choose not to follow God's commandments we have to live with the consequences.

Bible – What's in

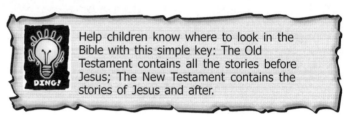

Main idea

The Bible is a collection of stories, poems, instructions, letters and plans about God and his people.

Questions answered

by this program

• So what's in this book called the Bible?

• Who is it all about?

Bible Base

Whole Bible.

For the leader

The Bible taken as a whole book is the record of God's dealings with the people God specially chose to reveal himself to, the Israelites. It spans the history of these people from prehistoric times through to the coming of Jesus and the establishment of the church. which reached beyond the Israelites to other peoples. The focus is on the relationship between God and his people. Parts of the Bible also refer to future events.

This first program simply introduces the Bible as a book containing a variety of forms of writing such as story, letters, poetry, instructions and prophecy.

It is suggested that the children make a fridge magnet to take home. Small magnets suitable for gluing on the back of their decorated card are available from craft shops or you can make use of any advertising ones you get.

 Help children know where to look in the Bible with this simple key: The Old Testament contains all the stories before Jesus; The New Testament contains the stories of Jesus and after.

. . . .

 Open the pack

FAMILY TREASURES

Why? To introduce the different types of messages in the Bible and the idea that they all relate to God's people.

Needed: *A 'family treasure chest' containing a family photo album, a letter or card from one family member to another, a poem or song that is special for your family, a list of instructions for a family member, (like a 'to do' list) and an itinerary for a future family holiday or event.*

Unpack your family treasure chest. As you show each of the items talk about how they are all about your family and the relationships you have with each other. Each one is a different kind of writing (letters, poems, stories, etc) but all are about your family.

Comment: The Bible is a bit like a family treasure chest. It's all about God and the people who love him and are part of his family.

CIRCLE STORYTELLING

Why? To get across the idea that the Bible is a continuing story.

Form a circle. The leader begins a story with a single sentence and each child adds one sentence to the story. The story must finish with the last child.

Comment: Stories are fun to tell and read as well. The Bible is the most important book ever written. It tells the story of God and his people. There are love stories, adventure stories, suspense stories, war stories, letters and lots more.

Dig in

MAKE A BOOK

Why? To introduce the Bible as being all about God and his people.

Needed: *Appendix 4 enlarged, coloured brightly and cut, to make eight separate A4 book pages, masking tape.*

Hand out each prepared page to a pair of children. As you begin to talk about each page have the pair come up and attach their page to the previous one using strips of masking tape so that when all eight pages are attached it can be folded like a concertina with the cover page on the outside.

Introduce each page of the book by talking about the form of writing and give one of the examples listed on the page. Keep the examples brief. For example when talking about *Stories about God's people* say 'This story is about a girl called Esther who became a queen and was able to save all of God's people from being killed by the king.' Show where the story is in your Bible.

READ A STORY

Why? To find out what they already know about the Bible.

Select a story from the CEV Bible, such as Jesus in the synagogue from Luke 4:16-21, 28-30. Read it to the children then ask if they know any other stories from the Bible and talk about them together.

Comment: The Bible is full of stories about God and the people who love him and are part of his family. There are also letters, poems, instructions, and details of God's future plans for his people.

 # Chew on it

FRIDGE MAGNETS

Why? To consolidate the idea that the Bible is the story of God and his people and give them something to take away.

Needed: *A copy of Appendix 7 for each 6 children, cardboard, paste, felt pens, contact, small magnets (available from craft shops).*

Give each child a circle from Appendix 7 to decorate, paste onto cardboard and cover with contact. Finally stick a magnet on the back.

Close the pack

Comment: Some people have read the Bible right through many times and they still discover new things each time. Many read it everyday and they think it's the best book ever. The Bible isn't like any other book. It's not easy to get the story just by starting at the beginning and reading it through to the end. It contains amazing things for us to discover and we'll be able to do just that over the next few weeks.

Main idea

The Bible is God's Word to us. From it we can learn lots of different things about God and about us.

Questions
answered

by this program

- The Bible is about long ago – what's that got to do with me?
- What sort of stuff is in the Bible that might interest me?

Bible Base

Whole Bible.

The Book and Me

For the leader

This program introduces the Bible as God's Word for us and introduces some of the things the children may find inside. It aims to show that even though it was written a long time ago it is still relevant today for everyone.

To use the acrostic you will need to write vertically on eight sheets of paper, like this

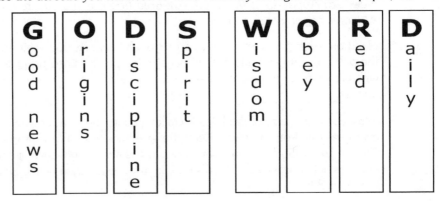

Keep the first letters the same size and distance from the top edge of the paper so that when the rest of each word is folded back, the first letters can be read across as GOD'S WORD'.

. . . .

 Open the pack

HUNT THE BOOK

Why? To get the children to think about different types of books and what the Bible might be for.

Needed: *10 or more different kinds of books such as a novel, a first aid book, a street guide, a travel book and a cookbook and a train timetable.*

Spread out the books around the room. Give each pair of children a list of the kinds of books to find. For example, A book to read for fun, a book to help when someone is hurt, a book to help me find my way...). The children need to find the book that matches what's on their list and write its name next to the description. Once one pair has finished go through the list showing the children the different books.

Comment: There are different books for different things. Today we will look at a very special and different book and what we can use it for.

OPEN IT

Why? To emphasis the idea that a closed Bible is no use to us.

Needed: *7 items from home that need opening before they can be of any use, such as an umbrella, drawer, atlas, banana, canned fruit and bottle of coke.*

> ***Show the items and pose the question:***
> *What do all these items have in common?*
> (They all need to be opened before they can be used.)

 **Dig in**

GOD'S WORD ACROSTIC

Needed: *Acrostic letters (See For the leader)*

Give the vertical words to eight children and use them to explore together some of the characteristics of the Bible. When you have finished, the children should be able to fold back all but the first letters and line them up to read 'God's Word'.

Good News	We can find out all about Jesus and God's plan to help us be his friends.
Origins	We can find out about how God made the world and us.
Disciples	We can find out about how Jesus wants us to be disciples.
Spirit	We can find out who the Holy Spirit is and what he does.
Wisdom	We can find out about God's way to be wise.
Obey	We can find out how obeying God is the best way we can live.
Read	If we don't open our Bible and use it, it won't do us any good!
Daily	Reading the Bible every day helps us to keep close to God and live his way.

GOIN' FISHING

Needed: *(For each group of 4-6) A bowl containing 8 fish shaped cards (about 10x5cm) each with one of the letters of 'God's Word' on one side and the corresponding description from the* God's Word Acrostic *activity on the other side.*
(G – Good News, O – Origins, etc) and a paperclip attached. A simple rod and string fishing line with a magnet attached.

Divide the group into teams of 4-6 children. Give each team a bowl of 'fish' and a rod. Play a fishing relay game in which the winning team is the one to collect all their fish and organise the letters into the right order to spell two words that tell us what the Bible is *(Gods Word)*.

Gather together and look at the descriptions on the back of the fish.

 Chew on it

OLD AND NEW

Why? To give a chance to correct any misunderstandings about the Bible.

Needed: *A board or large sheets of paper with the headings 'OLD' and 'NEW'.*

Form small groups and challenge the children to think of 5 things they already knew about the Bible and 5 things they have just learned. As the groups share their answers, list them under the headings. If they are slow coming up with 'NEW' things get people to share things they know about the Bible that they think others may not know.

 Close the pack

Pass your Bible around the group so each child gets to hold it. As they do this explain that the Bible is really lots of smaller books in one –like a library. Explain that you read the Bible regularly (daily if you do!) and that it helps you to get to know God and to find out how you can be the best that you can be with his help – it's a real life adventure!

Pray to God for help each week to discover more about his Word, the Bible.

Main idea

To begin to discover how to find stories in the Bible using book name, chapters and verses.

Questions answered

by this program

- What are these numbers all over the pages?
- How do I know where to look in the Bible?

Bible Base

Exodus 9:22-28
Luke 8:22-25

For the leader

We want children to become excited with the Word of God and develop the skills necessary to navigate through it. This will not happen overnight so the more practise children get at looking stories up for themselves with your help, the easier it will become for them. To give them a good start, you may like to recruit some extra helpers for this program so the children quickly find out how to do it. Pre-brief the leaders that it is not their role to find the place for the children but to help the children learn how to find it for themselves. This will involve helping them understand the parts of the reference that refer to the book, chapter and verse and showing them where these appear on a page.

The children will find Bible stories about storms as a way of exploring the structure of the Bible.

. . . .

 ## Open the pack

STORM IN A TEACUP

Why? To introduce the theme of storm stories.

Dramatically describe a storm or read a short storm story or poem and whilst doing this have the children find a space and pretend to be the wind, the rain, or someone you are describing so they get the feeling of the storm.

SINK THE BOAT

Why? To have fun and introduce the theme of storms.

Needed: Large bowl of water, paper boats, straws

Choose two contestants to place their boat in the water and 'make a storm' using only their straw placed in their mouth (no hands). The aim is to capsize/sink the opponents boat first. They may blow, splash, blow bubbles but they cannot touch the other boat. This game will make a bit of a mess so put a plastic sheet on the floor and have some towels to dry off with! Encourage the rest of the group to cheer the contestants.

Dig in

STORMS

Needed: Sign 'Exodus 9: 22-28'

> *Pose the question:*
> *If you wanted to find a storm story in the Bible, where would you look?*

Let the children suggest ways.

Explain that you have 'references' for three storm stories. A reference is a bit like an address that helps us find the place. Show a card on which is written 'Exodus 9:22-28'. Point to the relevant part as you say 'Exodus chapter 9 verse 22 to 28.' Invite anyone who knows how to use a Bible reference to explain about book, chapter and verse. The 'anyone' may need to be you or a helper! Show the table of contents page, which lists the names of the books. Give out the Bibles and let children find the contents page in their Bible.

CAUGHT IN A STORM

Why? To practice finding a Bible passage from its reference.

Needed: *A leader, a Bible and the 3 questions from Appendix 6,* Storm stories *for each team of 3-6.*

Seat the teams on the floor and have them choose three 'runners'. The first runner has to run to the main leader and collect the first of three references with the question. The team must look up the reference, read it and send the second runner back with the answer and to collect the next reference and question. The first team to answer all three questions correctly wins.

Talk about how they found the stories and what they discovered from reading them. Explain that once you can look up references, you can find any story in the Bible as long as you have its reference.

POWER OVER A STORM

Why? To get some idea of the process of looking up a Bible story from a reference.

Tell the story of the storm found in Luke 8:22-25. If you have time have the group do an impromptu acting out of the story as you tell it making sure everyone gets a role of some sort. Then show them how to look it up, finding first the book, then the chapter and then the verse. Read the story together, looking for something new.

Talk about how you found this story and what you discovered by reading it.

 # Chew on it

CODE IT

Why? To give practice in using the reference system.

In pairs or small groups, encourage the children to look at their Bibles and read random verses, then write down the reference for any verse they want. They should then swap references with those in the group next to them and see if they can find the verses.

EXPLORE

Why? To get used to handling the Bible and working with the big (chapter) and little (verse) numbers.

Ask the children to scan their Bibles to find

- a chapter that goes for more than two pages
- a chapter in the first half of the Bible with more than 50 verses
- a chapter with more verses than anyone else
- a chapter with fewer verses than anyone else
- two 'Chapter 5's.

 # Close the Pack

It's amazing that we can read about storms that happened long ago because the reference system helps us find all the stories in the Bible.

10

Main idea

The Bible is like God's biography. We can find out about what God has done by reading it.

Questions answered

by this program

- Where can I find out stuff about God in the Bible?
- What sort of stuff might I find out about him?

Bible Base

Whole Bible.

God's in the Book

For the leader

This Bible program gives the children the opportunity to practise their skills at looking up references by playing a board game. You will need a set of Bibles with clear print and easy-to-understand text. We recommend the Contemporary English Version (CEV). Sets of these are available at mission prices from most Scripture Union and Bible Society offices. You could offer your church or parents of the children the opportunity of making a donation towards these.

We want the children to discover lots of the characteristics of God and his relationship with his people in the Bible and be excited by what else they might be able to find there. As you prepare, look up the references for the board game and spend some time considering the character of God and his relationship with you. Pray that the children will capture your excitement as together you discover God in the Bible.

Coloured Post It notes are ideal for marking places in the Bible.

. . . .

 Open the pack

BIBLIOGRAPHIES

Why? To introduce the theme of biographies.

Show the group one or more biographies, preferably of people they would know about, such as Captain Cook or a famous sports star or actor. Discuss biographies saying that they tell us about a person's life and what they have done.

Comment: The Bible is a bit like a biography because it tells us lots about God. We can find out something new about him on almost every page.

PICTURE STORY

Why? To introduce the Bible as the true story about what God has done.

Choose a short factual picture biography and read it to the children. Briefly talk about what they discovered about the person from the story.

Comment: The Bible is the true story about God and today we are going to use it to find out some things about him.

 ## Dig in

RACE AROUND THE BIBLE

Needed: *A leader, a game board (Appendix 7), a set of game cards (made from Appendix 8) and a Bible for each team of about 4 children*

Play the game according to the instructions on the board. Encourage players to help each other if they are having difficulty, as the aim of the game is to be the first whole team to get all their players home. Should a group finish early they can play again with the cards they haven't already used.

GIANT RACE AROUND THE BIBLE

Needed: *22 rectangles of cardboard (the insides of large cereal boxes are ideal.) Write 'start' on one, 'home' on another and the numbers 2 – 21 on the rest. If you like, decorate the rectangles to make them more fun. Make up a set of cards from the Bible references found in Appendix 8.*

Place the large rectangles of cardboard, in order, in a snake shape down the centre of the room to form your game board. Divide into 2-4 teams and play according to the instructions on Appendix 7 with one child from each team being the 'counter' on the board who moves according to the instructions on the cards. The aim of the giant game is to be the first team to get their 'counter' to the 'home' square.

RACE TO THE PLACE

Needed: *6 or more of the Bible references from Appendix 8 written on a large sheet of card with separate pieces of paper attached with Blu-Tack covering each reference. A Bible for each pair of children.*

Each pair places their Bible in front of them on the floor, hands off. One by one, remove the strips of paper and call out the reference for the children to find. Choose a different pair each time to read the verse and tell the whole group what it reveals about God.

 ## Chew on it

Reward the winners of the game with a very small token (a sticker or lolly would be appropriate) and then reward everyone else in the same way commenting that one of God's characteristics is that he wants to treat everyone in the same way, – we can all be winners with God. Briefly talk together about what you have found out about God today.

Close the pack

Invite volunteers to offer a one-sentence prayer thanking God for the Bible or for what we know about God.

Encourage the children that they will find out a lot more about God from the Bible as they come to club each week.

Keep your program moving. Have all equipment at hand and know exactly what you plan to do next.

11

Main idea

Jesus is a most important person because through our calendar all the events in history are linked to his birth.

Questions answered

by this program

- What do BC and AD mean?
- When did Jesus live?
- What date was he born?
- Is Jesus a real person?

Bible Base

Matthew 2:1;
Luke 2:1-2

For the leader

Our system of dates is based on the birth of Jesus Christ. The initials BC and AD attached to a year refer to 'Before Christ' and 'Anno Domini', which means in Latin, 'in the year of our Lord'. The terms BCE (before common era) and CE (common era) are increasingly being used because the Christian system of dates is used both by Christians and non-Christians.

. . . .

 Open the pack

FAMOUS PEOPLE QUIZ

Why? To introduce the idea of Jesus being perhaps the world's most famous person.

Needed: Newspaper or magazine photos of famous or well-known people (Look for those your group will know reasonably well. For large groups show them on an overhead projector, otherwise make sure they are big enough for the children to see clearly.)

Don't tell the children you are about to show famous people. Show each person while children write down or say who it is. Ask the children what these people have in common.

Comment: Today we are going to talk about someone many believe to be the most famous ever. People call themselves by his name, build buildings because of him, and have followed his teachings for 2,000 years. Who do you think it is?

TIME LINE

Why? To establish the idea of the progression of time.

Needed: A sketch of Jesus in the manger , sketches of historic events the group will relate to such as Captain Cook visiting Australia, the opening of the school/church, Neil Armstrong walking on the moon and the Sydney 2000 Games. Include a future event such as next Christmas.

Arrange the sketches (minus the manger scene) in order and talk about the dates.

> *Pose the questions:*
> *How far back do dates go? Can dates be before zero?*
> (Yes, BC) *What does BC mean?* (Before Christ)

Add the 'Jesus in the manger sketch' to the timeline and let it sink in that our dates begin with the birth of Jesus.

> *Pose the question:*
> *What does that say about the importance of Jesus?*

 Dig in

Comment: The Bible is the key book for finding information about Jesus.
It tells what it was like in the world when Jesus was born.

Place in History

HISTORICAL FACTS

Let pairs of children find Matthew 2:1 and Luke 2:1-2 and read it to discover historical facts about the time when Jesus was born.

Comment: Other history books tell us about the time that Herod was the King, the emperor was Augustus, and Quirinius was governor. That's the time that Jesus was born. It was a real time in the history of the earth. The birth of Jesus was important enough that all the events that have ever happened have been linked to that day!

THE MOST IMPORTANT

Pose the questions:
What year is it this year? What does that number mean?
(That's the number of years since Jesus was born.)

Comment: Every time you write the year you're really remembering when Jesus was born and how long ago it was. That's how important Jesus is.

Chew on it

SING: JESUS IS GREATER

Needed: Gospelling to the Beat 1 *CD and player*

Sing the song or play the CD while the children clap. Get them to suggest actions and sing the song together.

SO WHAT?

Pose the question:
If Jesus really is the most important person who ever lived,
what should we do about it?

Encourage discussion, including things like 'find out as much as we can about him' and 'do what he says'.

Close the pack

MOST IMPORTANT

Pose the questions:
Herod was the king at the time, but who has heard his name mentioned recently?
Does anyone remember the name of the man who discovered that the world was not flat? (Columbus). What about the name of the person who invented the telephone? (Thomas Edison). Has anyone heard the name Jesus recently?

Comment: Jesus must be someone worth remembering because his name is still being talked about when many other important names have been forgotten. Jesus was born (2000) years ago, but we all know his name. He must be worth finding out about. That's what this club is about. We're here to find out about Jesus.

**Encourage everyone to come back next session,
saying you'll have a surprise for them.**

12

Who is Jesus? The On...

Main idea

Jesus is an important person because God promised he would come hundreds of years before he was born.

Questions answered

by this program

• Why is Jesus different to anyone else?

• What's a prophecy?

Bible Base

Matthew 2:3-6;
Micah 5:2;
Luke 4:16-19;
Isaiah 61:1-2

For the leader

The idea of time is difficult for little children so they don't readily grasp the importance of prophecies made hundreds of years before the event, however they can appreciate that God kept his word in sending Jesus. That Jesus is the Promised One, makes him very important.

It was suggested last session that you promise the children a surprise. Don't let anything prevent you from keeping that promise. It can be something as simple as a sweet or a sticker, something more special, like a Bible Society leaflet, or a cookie you've baked with a message inside.

. . . .

 Open the pack

WHO AM I?

Why? To establish what makes people important.

Divide children into groups, each group with a paper and pencil.
Ask the following questions about important people:

1. What is the name of the President of the United States?

2. Who is our Prime Minister?

3. What is his wife's first name?

4. Who is the captain of (choose a sporting team)?

5. What is the name of Australia's most famous bushranger?

Pose the question:
Why were these people important?
(Because of their position or for what they have done)

GUESS WHO?

Why? To establish what makes people important.

As children arrive pin the name of a famous person on their back. They have to discover who they are by asking the others questions that have a 'yes/no' answer.

Pose the question:
Why were these people important?
(Because of their position or for what they have done)

BABY FACE

Show a picture of a baby and ask, 'Is this a famous person?' 'Why don't we know?'

Comment: Very few babies, if any, are born important. They usually become important when they grow up because of a job they do or a title they get.

 Dig in

KEEP YOUR PROMISE

Ask, 'Who remembers the promise I made last week?'
Comment: Isn't it good that you've only had to wait one week!

who was Promised

God made a promise hundreds of years before it happened about a baby who would be very important. When Jesus was born, people already knew what he would do. God had made a promise hundreds of years before. Let's look at that promise before I keep my promise to you.

LOOK IN THE BIBLE

Why? To discover Old Testament promises fulfilled in Jesus.

Help everyone look up the following passages and follow as they are read by volunteers who are good readers or a leader.

Show a picture (perhaps on a Christmas card) of the wisemen who visited Jesus.

Read Matthew 2:1-6

Explain that when Herod the King found out that a special baby was going to be born he wanted to know where. They knew where because this special baby had been promised in a book called Micah written hundreds of years before. We can read the promise because it's in the Bible.

Read Micah 5:2

Comment: God's promise came true. But the promise was not just about where he would be born. It was also about what he would do – his life.

Read Luke 4:16-19

Comment: What Jesus read was something that was also written in the Old Testament hundreds of years before.

Older children could find the promise in Isaiah 61.

Chew on it

SING: JESUS IS GREATER

Needed: Gospelling to the Beat 1 *CD and player*

Enjoy this song complete with actions.

GOD'S BIG PROMISE

Pose the question:
If Jesus was God's big promise, what do you think we should do about it?

Resist the temptation to tell how important it is know Jesus. Encourage the children to think about and verbalise what their response to Jesus should be.

If you sense it is appropriate you could ask for a volunteer to pray that you will all get to know Jesus better.

Close the pack

Jesus is an important person because all the events of history are linked to his birth, also because God promised Jesus would come and he did.

KEEP YOUR PROMISE

Give each person their promised surprise saying, 'Just as God promised, he gave us someone special and important in Jesus. I can't ever give you something that special, but I'll keep my promise to you and I hope it reminds you of Jesus.'

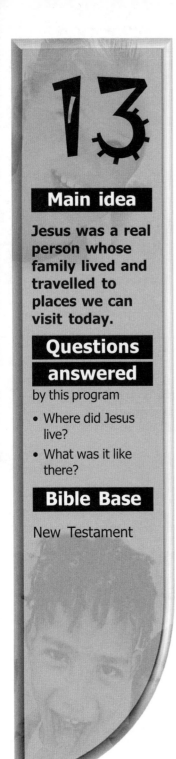

Main idea

Jesus was a real person whose family lived and travelled to places we can visit today.

Questions answered

by this program

- Where did Jesus live?
- What was it like there?

Bible Base

New Testament

For the leader

Young children sometimes have the idea that the Bible stories about Jesus took place in heaven, or some far off galaxy. This session establishes the 'earthliness' of it all by linking Jesus with real places he visited on earth. It will be much more real to your group if you show present day pictures of these places. Check out library books or brochures from travel agents, or photos taken by someone who has travelled in that part of the world.

. . . .

 ## Open the pack

WHERE IN THE WORLD?

Needed: World map or globe, Copy of Appendix 9, *Bible lands map.*

Explore a map of the world or a globe with the children seeing if they can find places you suggest – places which have been in the news. Find out if there are children in the group who were born overseas or whose family came from another country. Ask the following questions. Invite selected children to come and indicate their answers on the map/globe.

- Where were you born?
- Where were your parents born?
- Where would you like to go?
- Where did Jesus live when he was a man on earth?

Point to the area of Israel/Palestine on the map or globe, then use *the Bible lands map* to zero in on the area where Jesus lived.

SING *JESUS IS GREATER*

Needed: *Gospelling to the Beat 1 CD and player.*

Comment: The words of this song describe what Christians believe about Jesus. These things come from the Bible, the key book for Christians. Christians believe that Jesus is the most important person who has *ever* lived.

Don't forget the actions as you sing!

Dig in

JESUS' WORLD, OUR WORLD

Why? For the children to realise that the places mentioned in the Bible are real places on earth.

Needed: *Copy of Appendix 9,* Bible lands map, *present day photos of Bible land places.*

Display the map, saying that this is a map of the part of the world where Jesus lived. Explain that the Bible records the names of places Jesus visited, real places people still visit today. As you read these verses (or get volunteers to read them), ask the children to listen for the names of places mentioned and then find them together on the map and discuss the present day photos.

- Luke 2:1-4

- Luke 2:39-42

- Luke 4:31

- Luke 5:1

Choose volunteers to trace Jesus' journey, recorded in Matthew, on the map.

- Matt 2:1   Bethlehem

- Matt 2:14   Egypt

- Matt 2:23   Nazareth

- Matt 3:13   Jordan River

- Matt 4:23   all over Galilee

JESUS' JOURNEYS

Why? For the children to realise that the places mentioned in the Bible are real places on earth.

Needed: *Enlarged copy of Appendix 9,* Bible lands map

Form groups of 2-5 each with a Bible and the Bible lands map. Challenge the groups to look up the verses from Luke and Matthew mentioned above to find nine places Jesus visited or as many as they can in the time. As they find them they can mark them on the map.

 # Chew on it

Why? To help the group understand that although Jesus lived in places we can visit now, he lived in a different time so many things about those places have changed.

Comment: Jesus lived on the same earth we do. We could get on a plane and go to Bethlehem and Nazareth and Jerusalem today and some people do. They are real places.

Either in small groups or all together think of five things that would be the same about those places now and five things that would be different.

- **Same:** Lake, mountains, rocks, language, climate, animals

- **Different:** Cars, electricity, TV's, government, phones

 # Close the pack

Comment: Jesus is an important person because all the events of history are linked to his birth.

Jesus is an important person because God promised that Jesus would come years before he was even born.

Jesus is an important person because he did unusual things in real places we can go today.

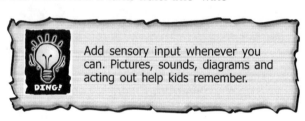

Who is Jesus? Both

Main idea

Jesus is a person who was both God and man.

Questions answered

by this program

- Can Jesus do magic?
- What did people think when they saw him?
- How does Jesus know how I feel?

Bible Base

John 2:1-11

For the leader

Jesus was God from the beginning (John 1:1) but he was also fully human. He faced the whole range of emotions and temptations we do (Hebrews 4:15). You could have passed him in the street without realising he was God because he probably looked much the same as others his age in his part of the world.

Children are often more ready to accept that Jesus was God than that he was an ordinary person. They love superheroes and are happy to accept an all-powerful Jesus, but an understanding of his humanity helps us relate to him as a friend.

If you can get hold of some Potassium Permanganate (better known as Condy's Crystals, available from chemists) try this for impact as you tell the story.

Use a clear jug filled with water and 2 empty glasses. Place 2-3 Condy's Crystals in the bottom of each glass. The children won't notice them but they are concentrated enough to turn the whole glass a purple colour At the appropriate time in the story pour water from the jug into the 'empty' glasses and watch how it turns water into 'wine'

 Add sensory input whenever you can. Pictures, sounds, diagrams and acting out help kids remember.

 Open the pack

GUESS HOW I'M FEELING?

Needed: Separate cards with the words 'sad', 'hungry', 'angry', thirsty', and 'tired'. Five separate faces from Appendix 10, Facial expressions

Divide the children into 5 groups. Give each group an emotion card and get them to develop a short role play about that word. Have each group in turn act out their role play while the others try to guess the emotion.

As each emotion is guessed, display the corresponding face.

SONG: JESUS IS GREATER

Needed: Gospelling to the Beat 1 CD and player, Copy of Appendix 10, Facial expressions, *cut into separate faces.*

Sing the song with actions. Afterwards pose the questions:

How do you feel when you sing that song?

Can you think of a song that makes you feel very differently?

Show the cartoons from Appendix 10 and identify the emotions.

> *Pose the questions:*
> *Do you think Jesus had feelings like us?*
> *Is there any evidence?*

God and Human

Comment: If we can find evidence of Jesus having feelings it will show he was human just like us. Let's check the Bible to see what we can find.

Dig in

You will need to choose activities that show BOTH that Jesus was human and that he was God.

CHECK OUT THE EVIDENCE

Needed: *Separate faces from Appendix 10, Blu-Tack, these Bible references written on separate cards, Bibles*

John 11:35, Mark 11:12, Matt 3:5, John 19:28, Mark 6:31.

Give each group a Bible reference card. They need to find the verse in the Bible, work out which emotion Jesus was experiencing, find the matching picture and display them together.

LIKE US

Invite the group to be detectives and find out how Jesus showed he wasn't just superhuman. He was like us in lots of ways. Read the above verses or ask volunteers to read. As each human emotion is identified, point to the corresponding cartoon. Point out that Jesus often felt like we do. He was a real person.

NOT JUST HUMAN

Tell the story of the wedding at Cana or read it from John 2:1-10. (You could do some ad lib dramatizing.) Make sure the children understand that this was no trick. Jesus is the Great Creator God and turning water into wine is nothing compared to creating the world.

Chew on it

Pose the questions:
What is there about that story that shows Jesus was different?

What would you have thought if you were there?

Comment: As you read other stories about Jesus you will discover that he did all sorts of amazing things. Ask the children if they know what else Jesus did, if not list some. (Use visuals to illustrate wherever possible.) Point out that Jesus was able to do these things, not by tricking people but because he was not just a human being, he was in fact the Son of God who had come to earth in human form.

Many people who saw these things believed in Jesus and followed him.

Read John 2:11 together and point out that when the disciples who were there saw Jesus do this amazing miracle, they put their faith in him and went with him.

Close the pack

Some people put their faith in Jesus when they saw what he could do. Others didn't like what he said and did. They became angry and would not believe. Jesus wants everyone to put their trust in him and follow him, not to be angry and unbelieving or uncaring and ignore him.

You or someone else might like to conclude with a prayer for understanding of who Jesus really is and for the ability to respond to him as he deserves.

Main idea

Anyone can follow Jesus. To get started, a person needs to accept his invitation.

Questions answered

by this program

- Is Jesus only interested in good people?
- How do you start following Jesus?

Bible Base

Matthew 9: 9-13

For the leader

Some leaders unnecessarily cloud the whole 'deciding to follow Jesus' process in secrecy by inviting children to 'stay behind', we recommend you talk openly and generally about how to start with Jesus, so everyone can think about it.

The Pharisees considered themselves superior for carefully keeping the law, and criticised Jesus for mixing with tax collectors, who didn't. But Jesus said these were the very people he came to invite to be his followers. Jesus particularly invites those in your group who don't measure up and know it.

Never remain alone with a child from your group. Always move to an area where others can see you.

· ·

 ## Open the pack

WHO'S THE LEADER?

Why? To give the children an experience of following.

Seat everyone in a circle. Choose a volunteer to leave the room while you choose a leader from the children left. This leader commences an action which everyone else copies. The volunteer tries to guess who is the leader.

INVITATIONS

Why? To introduce the concept of RSVP.

Needed: A party or other invitation.

Show the invitation and discuss these questions:

To what sort of events do you get invited? What is the best invitation you have received? What made it so good? What information do invitations have on them? What does the person receiving the invitation need to do?

 ## Dig in

COME WITH ME!

Why? To help the group understand what it might have been like for the disciples when Jesus asked them to come with him.

Once the children are settled, choose one child and issue this command, '(Michael), Come with me!' and lead the way outside. When outside give them a written invitation to come to kids club next week or to something else you are planning for the group. Come back to everyone and ask the child:

What did you think might happen when I said, 'Come with me?'

Why did you come?

Comment: Jesus issued that same command to some people long ago.

Getting Started

DRAMA: JESUS' INVITATION

Explain that there are two groups of people mentioned in this Bible story.

1. Pharisees – important men who were like lawyers. They knew God's laws and helped people keep them. They meant well, but sometimes the keeping of the law became more important than caring for people.

2. Disciples – followers of Jesus.

Set up your room to act out the Bible reading in two scenes.

Scene 1: **At Matthew's tax office**
Choose someone to be Matthew sitting at his table collecting taxes from another person.
Read Matthew 9:9 from your Bible and then choose someone to be Jesus and act out what happened.

Scene 2: **Later, at Matthew's home**
Choose two or three children to be Pharisees, a few to be disciples and have the same 'Matthew' and 'Jesus'. Everyone else is a party guest.
Read Matthew 9:10-13.

Chew on it

GETTING STARTED

Comment: Following Jesus is more than finding out about him. Jesus is still alive. He invites us all to get to know him through his Spirit. We can have Jesus as our invisible friend.

Tell about how and when you chose to accept Jesus' invitation. Invite the group to ask questions.

Give each child a plastic teaspoon with the letters 'TSP' written on it.

Explain that 'TSP' is the abbreviation for teaspoon and it also stands for 'Thank you, Sorry, Please'. It reminds us of a prayer we can pray to join Jesus' team of followers.

T Thank you for your love for me and that you invite me to follow you.
S Sorry for the things I have done wrong
P Please forgive me and help me to be a good friend of yours.

Suggest that sometime soon they take their spoon to a quiet spot and think about Jesus' invitation to follow and how they will answer. Invite them to tell you about it next time they see you.

THEME SONG FOR FOLLOWING JESUS

Listen to and/or learn one of these songs:

• It's an adventure, Choosing Jesus *Gospelling to the Beat 1*
• Jesus makes things new, Take a little step, Be on Jesus' team *Gospelling to the Beat 2*

Close the pack

Comment: Jesus said to Matthew, 'Come with me!' and Matthew chose to come.

Jesus said the same words to me and I chose to come.

Jesus is saying the same words to you. I wonder what your choice will be?

Assure everyone that you'd like to help them think about it some more and they only need to ask.

Following Jesus

Main idea

In this lesson the children will discover that sometimes it feels great to follow Jesus.

Questions answered

by this program

- Was Jesus ever a big hero?
- Were Jesus and his friends always serious?

Bible Base

John 12:12-19

For the leader

This whole session is set in an atmosphere of chaotic celebration, as it must have been on Palm Sunday when Jesus entered Jerusalem. Success will depend on you and all other leaders enthusiastically playing the part.

People were curious about Jesus and those who travelled with him. They had heard that Jesus raised Lazarus from the dead, and wanted to find out more about this man. As Jesus came to the city of Jerusalem, many people, probably including some who were in the city for the Passover holiday, went out to meet him. They seemed to see Jesus as a potential nationalist leader who would help them become independent of foreign powers.

John recognised that the disciples did not understand the significance of this event until after Jesus' death (John 12:16). They were enjoying Jesus' popularity.

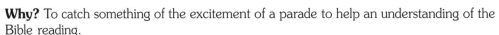

Open the pack

CREATE A STREET PARADE

Why? To catch something of the excitement of a parade to help an understanding of the Bible reading.

Needed: Streamers, materials to make flags (such as crepe paper or fabric, long cardboard rolls and tape), bright music

Choose some bright music to have playing while the children are creating their decorations. Use this time to ask questions like these:

Have you been at a festival or a street parade? What happened? Who looked like they were having the most fun? Who would you like to be in a parade?

Let as many as time allows, pretend they are a famous person and walk in front of all the children while they wave their streamers and flags.

Dig in

A BIBLE PARADE

At some stage during your parade celebrations tell the children to freeze in their position as you read John 12:12-13. Read verse 13 again as they unfreeze and begin cheering again.

Instruct them to freeze again as you complete verses 14 & 15.

SONG

Comment: When followers of Jesus get together one of the things they like to do to celebrate is to sing. Let's celebrate that Jesus loves us and we can follow him.

Choose a favourite song and sing it.

When it's Great

CELEBRATION PARTY

(Especially for groups who don't enjoy singing)

Bring along some snacks and have a party to celebrate that Jesus loves us and we can follow him.

 ## Chew on it

WHAT'S SO GOOD ABOUT JESUS?

Why? To help the children process and express their thoughts about Jesus

You might like to explain that on 10 June in the year 2000, millions of people across the world went in a Global March for Jesus. Many cities and towns across Australia have Easter Marches each year to celebrate that Jesus is alive.

> *Pose the questions:*
> *Why do they do that? What's so special about Jesus?*
> *(You might like to write a list of the answers and encourage the group to use them in the prayer activity.)*

PRAISE TIME

Alternate words and phrases mentioned in the above activity with 'J-E-S-U-S' to make a chant of praise. For example, 'J-E-S-U-S Awesome, J-E-S-U-S loves us, J-E-S-U-S powerful, J-E-S-U-S the best!'

 ## Close the pack

When you love Jesus and follow him, it's great to be with others who do the same. That's why people belong to churches. (Take the opportunity to invite the children to Sunday school or tell them about other kids programs at local churches and encourage them to go.)

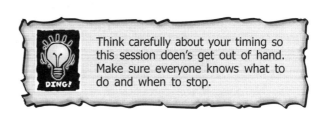
Think carefully about your timing so this session doen's get out of hand. Make sure everyone knows what to do and when to stop.

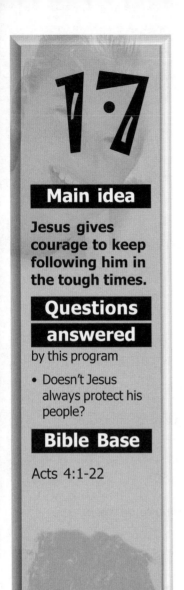

Main idea

Jesus gives courage to keep following him in the tough times.

Questions answered

by this program

- Doesn't Jesus always protect his people?

Bible Base

Acts 4:1-22

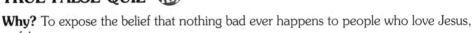

Following Jesus

For the leader

Following Jesus is not insurance against bad things happening. Jesus faced tough times and so do his followers, however, we know that overall God is in control. Even if the worst happens, we are eternally safe with him in heaven.

. . . .

 Open the pack

TRUE FALSE QUIZ

Why? To expose the belief that nothing bad ever happens to people who love Jesus, as false.

Designate the front of the room 'true' and the back 'false'. Read out the following statements and tell the group to move to the front or back of the room depending on whether they believe it to be true or false.

- According to the Bible, Jesus was born in Bethlehem. (T)
- There are millions of people who follow Jesus today. (T)
- All followers of Jesus live in western countries. (F)
- Some of the Bible was written before Jesus was born. (T)
- Jesus only wants good people to follow him. (F)
- The Bible says God existed before anything else. (T)
- If you follow Jesus nothing bad will happen to you. (F)

SONG FOR BAD TIMES

Why? To help children learn the song and the concept that God is with his people in the bad times.

Needed: Gospelling to the Beat 2 CD and player, song words (optional)

Play 'Song for bad times', encouraging the children to listen carefully to the words and say 'Boo Hoo' whenever they hear anything sad. Play it again saying 'Boo Hoo' at the end of the first two lines and 'Hooray' at the end of the second two.

Comment: Someone who loves God very much and has been a follower of Jesus for a long time wrote this song.

> ***Pose the questions:***
> *Do you think anything bad ever happened to the songwriter?*
> *What's the great thing about following Jesus when bad things happen?*
> (Jesus loves us and will be with us.)

 Dig in

A BAD TIME

Needed: *The following questions on a board or large sheet of paper, Bibles*

- Did everyone like them? Who didn't and why?
- What happened to Peter and John? Where did they spend the night?
- What happened that Peter and John would have been pleased about?
- What instructions did the officials give to Peter and John when they were released from prison ? Were they likely to get into trouble again? Why?

When it's Tough

Explain that even in Bible times bad things sometimes happened to Jesus' followers. Jesus called Peter and John to follow him. After Jesus went back to heaven they became important apostles. An apostle is someone chosen by Jesus to take his message to others.

Pose the question:
Do you think things always went well for Peter and John?

Form groups of 2-5 each with one or more Bibles. Display the questions and challenge the children to find answers in Acts 4:1-4, 18-20. Share answers

Comment: I'm sure it was very tough for Peter and John to spend the night in prison. And their only crime was telling people the good news about Jesus!

IN PRISON

Tell or read the story of Peter and John being put in prison from your CEV Bible. Ask the above questions.

Chew on it

WITH US IN THE TOUGH TIMES

Needed: Paper and pencils

Comment: We may never end up in jail, but we have tough times too.

Encourage everyone (leaders included) to write or draw about a tough time they are experiencing at the moment or might experience.

Have everyone scrunch up their paper and hold it in their hands. Invite those who wish to pray a sentence thanking God for being with them in the tough times and asking for help to keep on following.

JONI'S STORY

Tell the story of Joni Eareckson who became a quadriplegic when she was seventeen. She had been very active and independent but dived into Chesapeake Bay one hot summer day and hit the bottom. Suddenly she was helpless, totally paralysed from the neck down. She couldn't feel anything and couldn't move. Her sister came and carried her up onto the sand. Joni could tell that onlookers were very worried about her. 'Don't worry. I'll be all right. God won't let anything bad happen to me.'

The ambulance took her to hospital where she was operated on but they couldn't make her better. Joni had no feeling in her arms or legs. Over the next days and months she discovered she had broken her neck and was never going to be able to lead a normal life again. She was angry with God and cried bitterly. How do you think you'd feel if you couldn't move at all?

Gradually she learned to trust God again even though he had allowed that to happen to her. Joni is now more than 50 years old. She still can't move any part of her body below her neck but she's learned to write and paint using her mouth instead of her hand and she travels the world telling people that God will be with them in the tough times and help them through.

Close the pack

Comment: Tough times don't last forever, but Jesus never, ever leaves us.

18

Main idea

Every follower has a part to play in Jesus work on earth.

Questions answered

by this program

- What do I have to do if I start to follow Jesus?
- How will I know what to do?

Bible Base

Hebrews 10:25;
Phil 4:6;
2 Tim 3:17;
Matt 28:20;
1 Thessalonians
5:17

Following Jesus

For the leader

It's helpful to use different word pictures at different times when talking to children about life with Jesus. Some of these include, 'following Jesus', 'being Jesus' friend', 'belonging to God's family', and 'being a Christian'. This session uses the concept of 'being on Jesus' team'. Jesus' team consists of all who have said 'yes' to Jesus' invitation to come and follow him. Jesus' team has the task of doing what Jesus wants done in this world, under his coaching.

We are a Christian when we choose to accept what Jesus did for us and invite him to rule our life. Praying, reading the Bible, attending church and telling others don't make us a follower of Jesus but they help us be effective members of his team.

. . . .

 Open the pack

TEAM GAMES

Why? To give everyone a team experience.

Play some team games such as balloon tunnel ball or sock hockey.

FLASH INTERVIEWS

Why? To focus on what it means to join and belong to a team.

Ask everyone to ask as many people as possible in one minute if they belong to a team. They can keep count on their fingers. (This is chaotic but fun!) Restore order and share the results. Identify a few teams such as school sports or debating teams, gym squads or scout groups.

> **Pose the questions:**
> *How do you join these teams?*
> *Can anybody join?*
> *If you are part of a team, what do you have to do?*
> (Attend training, obey the coach, keep the rules)

 Dig in

MY PART

Why? So children will remember what good team members on Jesus' team do.

Needed: *Four large cards each with one of the letters in 'PART' on the front and the corresponding words and Bible references on the back (See below), TSP teaspoon from Session 15.*

Explain that Jesus has a team of followers.

Everyday

Pose the question:
What does it take to be part of Jesus team?

Talk about accepting Jesus' invitation to join. Show one of the TSP teaspoons from Session 15 and review how to accept Jesus' invitation.

Comment: Everyone who has accepted Jesus' invitation to follow him is on his team. As with other teams, there are privileges and responsibilities for team members.

Display the four cards with the letters P A R T in order.

For each one, allow some guesses as to what the letter might stand for before revealing the word on the back. After each word lead the children to read the Bible verse which reinforces the need to carry out our PART in Jesus' Team.

P	PRAY	1 Thessalonians 5:17, Phil 4:6;
A	ATTEND	Hebrews 10:25
R	READ	2 Tim 3:17
T	TELL	Matt 28:19, 20

Chew on it

LISTENING

Why? To affirm that Jesus invites us to be part of his team and to give those who haven't thought about their response yet a chance to do so. And for fun!

Listen to the song *Be on Jesus' team* from *Gospelling to the Beat 2*.

BRAINBUSTER

Why? To verbalise what they've heard about joining Jesus' team and to help you know what they understand. To give an opportunity for those who have joined the team to minister to those who are still thinking about it.

Pose the question:
If someone said to you 'Why should I join Jesus' team?' what would you tell them?

Close the pack

The best thing is that Jesus invites everyone to join his team. Assure everyone that you are happy to answer questions or talk to anyone who is thinking about joining Jesus' team but still isn't sure.

19

Main idea

Heaven is a wonderful place designed by God for those who love him.

Questions answered

by this program

- What's heaven like?
- What happens there?
- Is it boring?

Bible Base

Revelation 20:11-22:5, Hebrews 12:22-24a

The Ultimate Destination

For the leader

Children are usually full of questions about heaven whenever the topic is raised. The fact is, many of their questions, and ours too, have no definite biblical answers. This program involves exploring what the Bible actually says about heaven. Some of the verses touch on complex concepts. Don't be side tracked. The main point is that heaven is a wonderful place designed by God for those who love him. All who have accepted Jesus' invitation already have a party going on for them there and one day they will join in the celebration.

Mark 16:29 The guest of honour at a party always sat at the host's right hand.

. . . .

Open the pack

WHAT DO WE KNOW?

Why? To start the group discussing heaven and to raise their questions.

> ***Pose the questions:***
> *What do you think is the most interesting things about heaven?*
> *What would you like to find out about heaven?*

Comment: The Bible is the only place we can get reliable information about heaven because God is the only one who knows everything about it.

INVITATIONS

Why? To think about being invited to certain events to later lead into the fact that not everyone goes to heaven. We're invited and need to RSVP.

Needed: Invitations to various events

Talk together about invitations to special events and parties and the information that is usually included on an invitation like time, place, type of celebration and RSVP.

Dig in

SEE FOR YOURSELF

Why? To allow God to speak through his Word about heaven.

Needed: Bibles, 'HEAVEN' chart.

Display a chart like the one shown and allow the children to explore the passages individually or in small groups to discover what is most interesting for them. Share findings.

HEAVEN BOX

Why? To find out what the Bible says about heaven.

Needed: 'Heaven Box' (See below)

Show a decorated box which holds the following items with these Bible references on them. Choose children to remove one item at a time and guess what it might have to do with heaven, then choose a volunteer to read the reference.

> **HEAVEN**
> - A word picture (Revelation 21:1-8)
> - Like an amazing city (Revelation 21:11-27)
> - Where God and 'The Lamb' (Jesus) rule (Revelation 22:1-5)

The Heavenly Party

- Torch Revelation 21;11, 23; 22:5
- Death notices from a newspaper Revelation 21:4b, John 10:28
- Empty medicine or pill bottle Revelation 21:4
- Box of tissues or handkerchief Revelation 21:4
- Wanted poster or crime report Revelation 21:4b, 1John 3:15b
- Water bottle with your label 'PURE FRESH WATER' Revelation 22:1,2a
- A piece of fruit Revelation 22:2b, 3
- Cardboard crown Revelation 4:4, 10b, 11
- Pearl necklace or precious stone jewellery Revelation 21:19-21a
- Yellow cellophane Revelation 21:21b

 ## Chew on it

INVITATIONS

Why? To help the group think of what they have learned about heaven from the Bible in terms of a party.

Needed: Bibles, A4 paper sheets, felt pens

Have the children work in pairs or small groups to design an invitation for God's celebration party in heaven based on what they've discovered from the Bible. You could put these questions and references on a chart to help them.

- Where will it be? Heaven
- What will the venue be like? Revelation 21:16-21
- When will it be? Matthew 24:36
- Who will be there? Matthew 8:11, Revelation 7;9
- Music? (Think up a name for the group and include it on the invitation) Revelation 5:11,12
- Who is the guest of honour? Mark 16:19
- Food? Revelation 22:14, 22:2
- Drinks? Revelation 21:6, 22:17b

A sample invitation is in Appendix 11

INVITATION

Why? So each child knows they are invited to God's party.

Needed: A prepared invitation to the heavenly party for each child, felt pens

Give each child an invitation to decorate and write their name on.

 ## Close the pack

Needed: RSVP forms (Appendix 12)

Give each child a copy of the RSVP form. Talk about the different options.

Make sure that it's clear that heaven is for Jesus and all his friends and everyone needs to decide if they want to be there.

Suggest they take their RSVP away to think about and show you when they have filled it in.

20

Main idea

The angels in heaven celebrate over every single person who turns to Jesus.

Questions

answered

by this program

- Does everyone go to heaven?
- Will I go to heaven?
- Does God want me in heaven?

Bible Base

Luke 15:3-10

For the leader

We were created to celebrate with God forever. That's the reason Jesus' death and resurrection are so significant, because without them, we are cut off from God and our whole reason for existence is thwarted. No wonder heaven celebrates when we turn to God and are restored to God's intention for us for eternity. Although this life is by no means perfect for Christians, in one sense we have a taste of heaven now because our relationship with God is restored and we have the joy of living with him.

· ·

 ## Open the pack

HEAVEN – WHAT DO WE KNOW?

Why? To expose held views.

> **Pose the question:**
> *What do we know about heaven?*

Discuss whether the ideas came from the Bible or otherwise.

TREASURE HUNT

Why? To introduce the theme of seeking and finding.

Needed: Coins (real or chocolate)

Hold a treasure hunt to find the coins you have hidden around the room in advance.

 ## Dig in

LOST STORIES

Why? To discover that God wants more than anything for us to turn to him.

Needed: Bibles

Form two groups, each with a leader. Using Bibles one group will investigate Jesus' story of the Lost Coin (Luke 15:8-10) and the other the Lost Sheep (Luke 15:3-7). Groups should read the story then work out four 'photos' to present to the other group.

Instructions for 'photos'

Think about how the scene for each 'photo' might look. Decide who will be in it and how they should position their body. Those who are not going to be in the 'photo' can help by moving the limbs of those in the scene so they look just right.

Give a signal like 'Take your photo …NOW!' On the signal those in the scene assume their position for the shot. After each 'photo' ask those in it 'How were you feeling?' 'How did you show those feelings?'

Photo Shots
1. Where the person realises they have lost the coin/sheep.
2. Part way through the search
3. The moment they find the thing they lost
4. The gathering of friends to celebrate

Angel Party

STORYTELLING

Tell one of the 'lost' stories from Luke 15 dramatically.

Chew on it

COMPARING THE STORIES

Why? To bring out the point that there's a party in heaven whenever anyone turns to God.

> *Pose the questions:*
> *What was the reason for the celebration in each story?*
> *What does Jesus say is the reason for the celebration in heaven.*
> *What does it mean to turn to God?*
> (To give up doing our own thing and start pleasing God.)

LEADER TESTIMONY

Why? So the children will think about what their discoveries about heaven have to do with them.

Briefly tell about a time when you realised you were lost and away from God and turned back to him. Say what you're looking forward to about heaven.

Close the pack

THANK GOD

Why? To give a chance to review what has been learned about heaven and to respond to God's love for them.

Invite children to suggest things God's people can be thankful for when they think about heaven. Encourage those who wish to pray a thankyou sentence.

THE INVITATION

Why? So that children will know how to turn to God.

If you gave out the RSVP forms last week to take away and think about, focus on the second check box.

Comment: Jesus has prepared a place in heaven for all who turn to God. He takes us there when we die.

> *Pose the question:*
> *How do we know if we've turned to God?*
> (We've given up doing our own thing and try to please God)

Show your teaspoon and remind them of the **Thank you –Sorry – Please prayer** from Session 15.

21

Main idea

Jesus can help us to do what we should.

Questions answered

by this program

- What do I do when my friends are mean to me?
- How can I stand up to others?
- When should I do what others want me to?
- When should I not do what others want me to?

Bible Base

Romans 12:2; Proverbs 16:28; 17:9-17; 18:24; 22:24; 24:1

Peer Pressure

For the leader

Friendship can be negative as well as positive. Children need to learn how to handle these negative pressures and deal with them in positive ways.

Present Jesus to the children as someone who knows what it is like to be under pressure. He cares about them and will be with them as they go through difficult times in their friendships.

Jesus stood up to bullies (Luke 19:28-48; Mark 7:1-23). He cared about those who were being pushed around by others (John 4:1-42). He knows what it is to be let down by friends (Matt 26:14-16).

. . . .

 ## Open the pack

TASTE TEST

Why? To illustrate how easy it is to have our opinions changed by others.

Needed: *Small paper cups, two jugs marked Brand A and Brand B containing identical drink,*

Give everyone a taste from each jug and invite them to say which of two brands of drink they like best.

Beforehand, secretly ask a few influential people to deliberately choose brand A and subtly try to persuade the others to do the same one. Chances are the others will yield to this 'peer pressure' and choose Brand A.

Reveal that both drinks were the same and let people comment on the role of others in their choice.

Congratulate those who stuck to their own convictions.

FOLLOW THE LEADER

Why? To introduce the theme of doing what others do.

Appoint a leader and play 'Follow the Leader' moving around the room if possible or doing simple actions for the group to follow if in a confined space.

 ## Dig in

WHAT DO YOU DO?

Why? To think about how our friends sometimes influence us to do things we don't want to do.

Needed: *A copy of Appendix 13 cut into 6 'Situation cards'.*

Ask volunteers to choose a card describing one of the situations, read it aloud and pose the question 'What would you do?'

52

If you have extra time, groups of children could make up skits to act out the situations and a solution.

Pose the question:
Is it easier to say or do the right thing here than in real life? Why?

THE BIBLE ON FRIENDS

Needed: Bibles

Look up each reference with the children then discuss the question.

- What makes good friends? *(Proverbs 18:24)*
- What helps to keep friends together? *(Proverbs 17:9-17; 27:10)*
- What breaks up friendships? *(Proverbs 16:28)*
- What kinds of friends should be avoided? *(Proverbs 22:24; 24:1)*

Chew on it

DOING THE RIGHT THING

Why? To give children a strategy for working out what they should do and for doing it.

Needed: 'ASK' chart Appendix 14

Pose the question:
What can you say if someone asks you to do something you know is wrong?

List some useful responses like:

- 'I'm worried that you're doing something which is not good for you and I don't want to be part of it.'
- 'Let's do (something positive) instead.'
- 'I don't want to get into that sort of thing so I'm going.'
- 'I want to be your friend but I don't want to be involved in the wrong things you are doing. Call me when you decide not to do them.'

Display the ASK chart and discuss the three steps for saying no.

Pose the questions:
When is it good to do what other people want you to do?
When is it not good to do what other people want you to do?

(Refer back to the 'ASK' questions.)

Close the pack

Comment: It's often hard to go against what everyone else is doing, but sometimes we need to. We need Jesus' help to do the right thing and say no when others want us to do something wrong.

Jesus knows what it is like to be let down by friends and to be pressured (See *For the leader*).

Pray for the children and for yourself that you will all have the strength to stand up to negative influences and help your friends to do the right thing.

Body Image

Main idea

God made us, and even though we are different from each other, God says that each of us is very good.

Questions answered

by this program

- Why am I different?
- Am I OK?
- Does God love others better than me?

Bible Base

Psalm 139

For the leader

Older primary school children are becoming increasingly aware of their physical self and very few of them are happy with their bodies. But the Bible makes it clear that we, as humans, are created in the image of God and God likes what he made. (Genesis 1:31). God's image in us has been spoilt by sin, but God still thinks we are worth dying for. And God ought to know. Take every opportunity to offer acceptance and affirmation of every child in your group.

. . . .

 Open the pack

DRAW THE PERFECT BODY

Why? To open the topic of body image in a non-threatening way.

Needed: A4 paper sheets, pencils

Divide the children into groups of four, each with a sheet of paper. Instruct groups to fold the paper in half, and half again, to crease the paper into four horizontal strips. Unfold the paper. The first child in each group draws the perfect head on the top quarter of their page, but doesn't let the other members of the group see. This quarter is then folded behind and passed onto the next child who draws the perfect body of a man from the neck to the waist. This is quarter is folded under and passed on. Next child draws the perfect body of a person from the waist to the knee – including shorts for a boy and a skirt for a girl. The last child draws the perfect legs in the last quarter. Unfold the pages to see the 'perfect' bodies!!

SONG: GOD RECKONS WE'RE OK

Needed: Gospelling to the Beat 2 CD, CD player

Play the song and let the children sing along.

 Dig in

US AND GOD

Why? To discover that God knows all about us and is committed to us.

Needed: Bibles or Psalm 139 on acetate and overhead projector.

Display Psalm 139 using the Overhead projector or let the children find it in the Bibles. In small groups explore the psalm to answers these questions:

- What are some things that make the writer feel good about himself?
- Which verses does your group like best and why?

GOD AND US

Why? To discover that God knows all about us.

Needed: *Your Bible*

Comment: I wonder how much God knows about us. Listen as I read this part of the Bible to find out.

Read Psalm 139:14b-22.

 # Chew on it

EVERYTHING GOOD?

Why? To acknowledge that there are some things that are not good about us and we need to face them and ask God to help us overcome them.

> *Pose the questions:*
> *Might there be some things about us that God doesn't like?*
> *What sort of things?*
> (Bad things we've done, bad attitudes, unloving thoughts etc)

Comment: It's right that we should feel bad about ourselves when we do bad things. God loves us but he hates the bad things we sometimes do. He wants to take away all the bad in our life and help us be the people he created us to be.

VIDEO CLIP: BEAUTY AND THE BEAST

Why? To convey the idea that sometimes we have the wrong idea about ourselves.
We think we're ugly but being 'beautiful' involves more than the way we look.

Comment: Sometimes when we look in the mirror, we think we see a beast. Sometimes other people make us feel as if we are a beast. When God looks at us, he sees his beautiful creation that he treasures.

 # Close the pack

Every person is created by God and loved more than we can imagine.
God is committed to helping us have the best life possible with him.

SINGING

Play the song again. Choose some children, one at a time, and say to them,

'(Andrew), God made you and when he looks at you he sees what he has made and he thinks you're wonderful.'

23

Main idea

The Bible gives us clues about how to be a good friend.

Questions answered

by this program

- How can I find a good friend?
- How do I know if someone will be a good friend?
- Does the Bible talk about friends?

Bible Base

1 Corinthians 13: 4-8

Friends (1) What Makes

For the leader

The greatest love a person can have for his friends is to give his life for them (John 15:13). Jesus gave his life for us even though we were his enemies (Romans 5:10)

While very few young people will be required to give up their life for their friendships they will be called on to make hard choices at times. Jesus faced many of the difficulties young people face today and models the loving response in many situations. He was let down by his friends Judas, Peter and the others (Matt 26:14-16, 31-35, 46-56; Mark 14: 69-75) yet showed love to them and forgiveness.

Jesus understands young people today in their struggle in friendships and you can help them to see that the Bible has things to say about this area of their lives.

It's suggested that you take two sessions on this topic. It may be helpful to look at Session 24 as well as you plan this one.

. . . .

 Open the pack

FRIENDSHIP MAPS

Why? To help children think about their friends.

Needed: Paper and felt pens

FRIENDS

Give children paper and pens and ask them to draw a large stick figure in the centre of the page leaving room for smaller figures around the outside. Label the figure 'Me'

Ask them to think of their friendships and family relationships and draw their closest friends near 'Me', then those who are not so close further away. They could label the figures with initials.

FRIENDS

Invite them to draw a picture of themselves and their friends as above, not worrying about placement of friends in relation to themselves.

Be sensitive to children who seem to have no friends. They may like to include pets or toys in their maps.

Dig in

WHAT MAKES A GOOD FRIEND?

Why? To explore what the Bible says about real friendship.

Needed: Bibles, somewhere to list findings

Read 1 Corinthians 13:4-8 and ask the group to give you words from these verses which describe good qualities for a friend. List the words on sheets of paper or a board.

 ## Chew on it

THIS IS WHAT IT'S LIKE

Why? To apply the Bible teaching

Form groups of 2 –4. Let each group choose a word or phrase from the list without telling other groups and make up a skit to illustrate it. (Depending on the abilities of the group you may have to give them suggestions.) Let the groups present their skits for the others to guess the word or phrase.

MEMORY VERSES

Why? To remember specifics of being a good friend.

Needed: Memory verse cards below.

Give 14 children a memory verse card (or if you have fewer children, let them arrange the cards in order on the floor). Using a Bible let the children arrange themselves in the order the words appear in 1 Corinthians 13: 4-8. (You will need to help younger ones.)

Start by everyone saying together: 'Love is …' followed by people say their word or phrase, in order.

Have several turns getting faster each time.

 ## Close the pack

Pose the question:
How could you be a better friend this week?

If you used the memory verse cards the children could use them to pray for specific help to show those qualities to others.

| kind | patient | never jealous | never boastful |

| never rude | isn't selfish | isn't quick tempered |

| doesn't keep a record of wrongs that others do |

| loyal | hopeful | always supportive |

| trusting | never proud |

| rejoices in the truth but not in evil |

24 Friends (2) Being a

Main idea

Jesus can help us to be a good friend.

Questions answered

by this program

- How can I be a better friend?
- What stops people being friendly?
- How should we treat those who are not our friends?

Bible Base

1 Corinthians 13:4-8

For the leader

This session builds on the previous one and gives your group the chance to revisit the qualities of true friendship.

Some children struggle with friendships. Make sure the emphasis is on 'Being a friend' rather than 'Having friends'. Because children live very much in the present they sometimes change best friends frequently. Encourage them to be the best friend they can to everyone, even when others are not always friendly towards them.

When he was on earth, Jesus befriended people who were left out and shunned by others. He invites us all to be his friends, but particularly those who may have been let down by earthly friendships.

. . . .

 Open the pack

FRIENDS CHART

Why? To tap into children's experience of changing friends.

Needed: *Materials for chart*

Draw up a chart on a large sheet of paper, board or on OHP.

Friend	Not Friend

Suggest words and phrases for each column to describe someone who is a friend and someone who is not a friend. Be prepared for swear words and decide in advance how you are going to cope with this.

Discuss these questions:
How could a 'Not friend' become a 'friend'?
How could a 'friend' become a 'Not friend'?
Why do we need friends?

'HI FRIEND!'

Play bright music while everyone walks around giving high 5's. When the music stops each person must tell the last person they 'high5ed' something good about being a friend.

58

Good One

 ## Dig in

WHAT MAKES A GOOD FRIEND?

Why? To recall 1 Corinthians 13: 4-8

Needed: *Memory verse cards from last session.*

Pose the question:
What makes a good friend?

Refer to last session and 1 Corinthians 13: 4-8. If you didn't use the memory verse activity, now might be a good time to do it. If the group enjoyed it last week, why not have fun with it again?

Talk about the word 'love' and how we use it to mean different things. Explain this word 'agape' which the Bible uses to mean 'love' in this passage is not a feeling but a choice. We can choose how we act and what sort of a friend we will be, even to people who are not friendly towards us.

 ## Chew on it

ACROSTIC POEM

Why? To think about some of the qualities of friendship.

Needed: *Paper and pencils*

Encourage the children to work in small groups to make an acrostic based on the word 'FRIEND' for example

Find a good friend who
Respects your opinions
Interested in what is happening to you
Encourages you
Nearly always helps you out
Doesn't say bad things about you

ADVERTISING POSTER

Why? To think about some of the qualities of friendship they can offer others.

Needed: *Sheets of paper and felt pens*

Make a poster advertising yourself as a good friend. List qualities you are offering others. You might encourage them to add a note on it saying that they mightn't be all those things at present but they're trying.

 ## Close the pack

Jesus gave us a good guide for how to treat our friends – in fact everyone.

Ask children to find Matthew 7:12 in their Bibles.

Pose the question:
How do you like your friends to treat you?

Accept answers from the group such as 'kindly', 'including me' 'not being mean'.

Pray or ask a volunteer to pray that God will help you all be a good friend to others.

25

Main idea

When death occurs people experience many emotions. This is normal. Jesus understands because he experienced them too.

Questions answered

by this program

- Does God make people die?
- Am I going to die too?
- What's it like when people die?

Bible Base

Ecclesiastes 3:1-2; Ecclesiastes 9:1-12; John 11:1-35

Good grief

For the leader

When death comes to a family, adults are often so caught up in their grief that the needs of the children in the family are forgotten. At the worst they are totally ignored and this leaves the children confused. Many adults are reluctant to talk with children about the subject of death. Usually the children do not have anyone to sit down with them and explain point by point what has happened. When children can talk about death freely they are more likely to face it in a healthy way.

Teachers and other adults must not interfere with the grieving process by refusing to answer questions, making negative nonverbal responses or using diverting techniques. Children in their simplicity and spontaneity can handle grief far more naturally than adults. If they are not allowed to grieve, serious emotional and relationship problems may occur later in life.

'Life' has gone when someone dies. It will not come back. Death is a part of life. All living things eventually die. (Ecclesiastes 9:2, 5-6, 10-12). At death the body is not needed any more and has to be buried. God know what to do with the life that is gone.

Grief is experienced when the 'life' goes out of any relationship. Divorce, friends moving away, even giving up a loved activity can cause grief but these issues are not specifically tackled in this session.

A story is a good way to approach this topic. *The Cherry Blossom Tree* (Scripture Union), an illustrated story answering young children's questions about death is an excellent one. Ask for it at your local Christian bookshop or Scripture Union in your state or you should be able to find an appropriate story for your group at the local library. *The Very Best of Friends* (M. Wild and J. Vivas), *The Saddest Time* (N. Simon), *I'll Always Love You* (H. Wilhelm) and *Water Bugs and Dragon Flies* (Doris Stickney) are useful.

Children and Grieving is an excellent book from Scripture Union, for adults helping children through this issue.

. . . .

 Open the pack

DEAD OR ALIVE?

Why? To introduce the theme of living and dying.

Have a list of 20 people. Read out each one in turn and invite the children to respond by running to one wall if the person is dead or the opposite wall if they are alive. (Alternatively ask them to sit for one and stand for the opposite.)

EVER ALIVE?

Why? Because young children don't naturally understand the difference between living and non living things.

Needed: *A collection of natural objects such as a stone, a nest, a live grub, a pot plant, a leaf and a dead beetle.*

Talk about which items are alive, which were alive and have died and which were never alive.

 **Dig in**

WHAT DOES IT FEEL LIKE?

Why? To allow the children to express their response and hear other responses.

Needed: *5 signs*

Being very sad	Being angry	Pretending

Trying to change things	Getting life back to normal

Pose the question:
What does it feel like when someone you know dies?

Briefly talk about how you felt when a person you knew, or your pet, died. Think of a word to describe your feelings.

Ask the children if they can think of a time like that. If not, they might like to imagine how it might feel.

Ask each child in turn to write a word to describe their feelings on a large sheet of paper or white board. If they wish they may 'pass'.

Look at responses together and read them out. Ask if there could be other feelings.

FIVE STAGES OF GRIEF

Summarise the five stages explaining that these are stages children and adults normally go through. Put up the appropriate sign as you talk about it.

1. **Being very sad.** Feeling that you don't want to do anything, not able to eat or eating too much. No energy, feeling like giving up, thinking and saying 'if only'...

2. **Being angry.** Angry that the person has died. Angry with God for taking that person away. Asking lots of 'Why' questions.

3. **Pretending.** Not wanting to believe that this has really happened. Some people start to live in a make believe world where they believe that they will wake up tomorrow and the person who died will be back (or their pet will have come home) and everything will be fine again.

4. **Trying to change things by something you do.** Some people pretend to be sick to try to make that person or pet come back. Others act really good for the same reason.

5. **Getting life back to normal.** After the first four stages follows Stage 5 when eventually the person accepts that the death has really happened and it can't be changed and they start getting used to living without them. This can take a long time.

Dig in

IT HAPPENED TO JESUS

Why? So the children will know that Jesus experienced grief, so he understands.

Needed: *Bibles*

Summarise the story of when Jesus' friend Lazarus died *(John 11:1 – 31)* to set the context for what the children will read.

Read John 11:32-35 together.

Chew on it

JESUS UNDERSTANDS

Why? To emphasise the fact that Jesus experienced grief, so he understands.

> ***Pose the questions:***
> *How was Jesus feeling when he heard his friend Lazarus had died?*
> *Why was Jesus crying?*

Close the pack

Death is a part of life. Read Ecclesiastes 3: 1 and 2. God intended for us to live and knew that we would die. Just because we know that we will die one day doesn't mean that we don't feel sad when it happens to people we love.

Jesus felt very sad when his friend died just like we do. He understands how we feel when someone dies or big changes happen in our lives. We can talk to him even when no one else will listen and know that he cares and that he will help us. It is OK to feel sad and OK to cry. When we cry the tears have special chemicals that help us to relax and feel better. God invented tears for us to cry when we feel sad.

Ask a volunteer to pray thanking Jesus that no matter how bad things get, he will never leave us.

An additional activity for a group that is grieving

If you are using this program at school in response to the death of someone known personally to the children in your group, it may be wise to let the school know. Similarly parents of grieving children should be told when you intend to handle this sensitive issue. Such parents could be invited to be present so if the child wishes to discuss it with them, they will know what the child has heard.

Explain that when someone dies it is good to talk about the good memories we have of that person.

Give children a piece of paper and invite them to think about some of their memories of the person or pet who has died. Show them how to divide their paper into 4 or 6 squares and draw a picture, or write about the particular memory.

Ask the children to share their pictures and memories with one other person or with the group but don't force them.

(If children don't have anyone who has died ask them to draw some memories of their pets or grandparents, they would like to remember forever. Alternatively they may like to draw things they have been told about someone who died that they didn't meet, such as a grandparent, aunt or uncle.)

26

Are You Receiving?

Main idea

God want us all to be in communication with him.

Questions answered

by this program

- Does God ever communicate with people now?
- Will God hear me if I talk to him?
- Can anyone talk with God?
- What sort of things can talk to God about?

Bible Base

1 Samuel 3:2-11

For the leader

Children sometimes regard prayer as something very religious and strange, that's why this program seeks only to introduce the idea of 'talking with God', avoiding the words 'praying' and 'prayer'. Equating prayer with talking with God can be hard for us all. As you prepare this program spend some time reading some Old Testament conversations with God, like those in Genesis 18:20-33 and Exodus 3, and try to see them as prayer.

Note that we are concerned with talking *with* and not just *to* God. Prayer is not just talking with God but also listening to God. The fact that God speaks back in a variety of ways is crucial to an understanding of prayer.

. . . .

 Open the Pack

CHINESE WHISPERS

Whisper a message to someone, who whispers it to the next in line. The last person says it aloud to see how close it is to the original.

Comment: It's easy get the message wrong if we don't listen carefully and pass it on accurately.

Suggested message: 'Listen well, concentrate hard and pass on exactly what you hear and the end will be the same as the beginning.'

HUNT THE LOLLIES

Needed: A bag of sweets with enough for everyone.

Choose a volunteer to go outside with a leader. Hide the unopened packet of lollies somewhere in the room and instruct the rest of the group to guide the volunteer to the lollies using the words 'hot' and 'cold'. Meanwhile the volunteer has been instructed not to listen at all to the group's instructions! After a minute stop the game and talk about what happened.

Play again with the volunteer following directions. When the lollies are found share them with the group.

Comment: This play is about someone who had trouble knowing what was being said until they listened very carefully.

Dig In

PUPPET PLAY OR DRAMA

Needed: *5 copies of Appendix 15, Samuel and Eli Script and costumes for Samuel and Eli or two simple puppets. (You can make a puppet from a wooden spoon with a stick strapped across the 'chest' for arms, some simple clothing and a face drawn on the spoon.)*

Ask five volunteers to present the script. (If possible allow the characters to read through the script in advance.)

 # Chew on it

Comment: Samuel knew how to listen and talk to *Eli* but he found it strange to listen and talk to *God* at first. Some people find the idea of communicating with God a strange one.

> **Pose the question:**
> *What sort of things can we say when we talk to God?*

TALK WITH GOD HANDS

Why? Something to take away as a reminder.

Needed: *Small paper plate for each child, hole punch, ribbon, felt pens, ready made 'Talk with God hand'.*

Show your 'Talk with God' hand and let the children make their own to take home. Talk about the meaning of the word on each finger.

'TALKING WITH GOD' BALLOONS

Why? To encourage those who talk to God to share with the others.

Needed: *Balloons and permanent markers*

Mention some of things you talk with God about then invite others to do the same, being as specific as possible.

Draw out the words 'praise', 'sorry', 'thanks' and 'ask' and 'listen'.

Give the children balloons to blow up, tie off and write a simple sentence to God. Gather the balloons together in a bundle.

Comment: This bundle of balloons represents our groups' conversation with God. We don't have to wait until we hear God talking. We can talk to God confident that he hears and answers us if we are ready to listen to him.

Close the Pack

Comment: We call talking with God 'prayer' and when we talk to God we are 'praying'. When we know and love God it's a very natural thing to do, but even if you don't, it's a way of getting to know God. You can pray whenever you like, just like you'd talk to a friend. You can talk aloud or just think your prayers in your head.

Declare a one minute 'talk with God time'. Encourage all the children to talk silently with God. They could tell God how they feel, say sorry if they have done something they shouldn't have, thank God for something good he has done for them or ask God to help them or a friend. You might then have a time for each person to say a sentence aloud to God. (They might like to say aloud what they wrote on the balloon.) Then encourage them just for a moment to listen and see if God says something to them. Invite any children who think they 'heard' God, to tell you about it after. Close the session with a prayer for the children.

2·7

Main idea

One reason people are part of a church is to learn about Jesus.

Questions answered

by this program

- Why do people go to church?
- What's it like in church?

Bible Base

Luke 4:14-22

Why Church?

For the leader

This session and the next seek to de-mystify the Church through looking at its function and role. We want children to come away thinking that church is something they could easily be part of. 'Church' can be both the people and the buildings in the same way as 'school' can.

Jesus would have gone to his local synagogue (or meeting place) as a boy. There were no paid ministers, but the synagogue authorities would invite people to read and explain the Scriptures.

. . . .

Open the pack

WHAT HAPPENS INSIDE?

Why? To expose some of the wrong ideas children may have about church.

Divide the children and leaders into three groups:

- Group 1 – those who never go to church
- Group 2 – those who go to church sometimes
- Group 3 – those who go to church nearly every week.

(Make sure the children are not made to feel good or bad for belonging to any particular group.)

Invite each group in turn to stand out the front and answer questions like these:

1. What do you wish you knew about church? What do you think happens there?
2. What do you find strange about church? What do you like best?
3. What is church for? What are your favourite things about church?

SUNDAYS

Why? To introduce church going as one of the ways some ordinary people (like you) choose to spend Sunday.

Pose the question:
What do you usually do on Sundays?

Invite children to play charades to show what they do. Briefly act out your church experience.

Dig in

Comment: 'Church' is done differently in different places. In Bible times, the village synagogue or meeting place was a bit like church. The Bible tells what happened there one day.

66

WHEN JESUS WENT TO CHURCH

Why? For the children to discover that surprising things can happen in church.

Needed: A least two Bibles

Direct people to move into position as if they were in the meeting place, with boys on one side of the room and girls on the other. Appoint two excellent readers to be the narrator and Jesus who stand out the front and read Luke 4:14-22, 28-30.

Pose the question:
What surprising thing happened while the Bible was being read in that 'church'? (Jesus told them he was the one that the Bible was talking about – the one God would send to start to put things right.)

Chew on it

Needed: A cardboard sign with 'WOW on one side and 'Church' on the other.

Show the 'WOW!' Card. **Comment:** That was a real 'Wow!' moment for everyone in church that day. Sometimes when we learn about Jesus or God as we can in church, we have 'Wow!' moments when we realise something amazing that we'd never thought of before.

Share a 'Wow' moment of your own from a church-based experience.

'WOW!' MOMENTS

Why? To encourage children to expect God to be there and make himself known to them. To allow those who have experienced that in church to share.

Pose the question:
What have you heard about Jesus or about God that has made you think 'Wow, I didn't know that before'?

Explain that we can miss those moments if we're not looking for them. Encourage them to think about the *meaning for them*, not just facts about God. You might pray that you will all experience such times.

HAS GOD BEEN THERE?

Why? To encourage children to expect God to be there and make himself known to them. To allow those who have experienced that in church to share.

Pose the questions:
Have you ever been in church and known God was there even though you couldn't see him? What about another place? How did you know?

Close the pack

Comment: The people in the Bible reading had a 'Wow' time as they listened to Jesus that day in their 'church'. We can find out about Jesus in lots of places today like Religious Education in schools, SUPA club, Sunday School and church. But the church is where people who really know Jesus get together. That's a good place to go to hear the Bible read and explained.

(You might challenge older children to read their Bible during the week expecting God to give them 'Wow!' moments.)

28

Main idea

The church exists to reach out to the community with God's love.

Questions answered

by this program

- What else do church people do except sing and read the Bible?
- Why are there churches?

Bible Base

Acts 4:32-35 and Acts 6:1-7

For the leader

Two facts characterised the life of the first Christian community. Firstly, despite its size it had a common mind and purpose: it was united in its devotion to the Lord. Secondly, property was for the use of the community as a whole. These two characteristics broadly correspond to the two great commandments of loving God and loving others.

. . . .

 Open the pack

SHARING ACTIVITY

Why? To experience unfairness in sharing resources.

Needed: *Plates and biscuits (See below)*

Form groups of 6 – 8. Seat each group in a circle around a plate with one special chocolate biscuit, two cream biscuits and three dry biscuits. Tell each group that this is the food for their group today and that they can help themselves.

> **Debrief:**
> *What did you have to eat?*
> *Were you happy about that?*
> *What would you have wanted if you had the choice?*

Comment: The world is not fair. God hates unfairness and he's given his church the job of doing something about it.

NOBODY MISSING OUT

Why? To show how things can be held in common and divided up so no one misses out.

Needed: *A bag of sweets with enough for everyone.*

Seat everyone in a circle and hand out the sweets, several to some people and none to others.

> **Pose the questions:**
> *Is this fair? How could we make it fair?*
> *Have everyone with sweets put them in the centre and each person take just one.*

If you are running a SUPA Club or other non-church based group...

... think about how you can help the kids in your group make connections with a local church. Would they be welcome at a Sunday school social activity? Could you arrange a joint social activity like the JAFFA Do on page 6? What about a visit to one or more local churches or the chance to question kids and adults who attend?

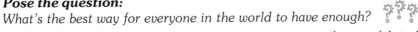

Our neighbourhood

 ## Dig in

SHARING FAIRLY

Why? To discover the biblical model of sharing.

> **Pose the question:**
> *What's the best way for everyone in the world to have enough?*

In small groups discuss the question and arrive at a group answer then read Acts 4:32-35 to discover how people made sure everyone had enough when the church first began.

JUST WHAT WE NEED

Why? To discover the biblical model of sharing

Explain that when the church first started they had a good way of making sure no one missed out on what they needed. Ask everyone to listen for how they did it as you read Acts 4:32-35.

Chew on it

Needed: *Examples of locally operating welfare programs*

Comment: Making things fair is God's plan for the church. Churches today have welfare programs for those who don't have enough.

Ask children if they know of local examples of the church caring for the needy. Examples might include Christmas toy appeal, hostels for the homeless, Meals on Wheels, and retirement homes.

PREACHING AND CARING

Why? To explore the place of caring for the needy amongst the other roles of the church.

Comment: As the church grew it became harder to divide things up fairly. The leaders were spending more and more time handing out food when there were other important things to do as well.

Divide the children into small groups and challenge them to find out how the church overcame the problem by reading Acts 6:1-7.

> **Pose the question:**
> *From this passage, what important things should churches do?*
> (Care for the poor and spread the message about Jesus.)

Note that the Salvation Army, St Vincent de Paul, Wesley Mission, Anglicare, and other similar organizations are church based and are the result of many churches of the one denomination joining together to do things they couldn't do as well as individual local churches. World Vision, Compassion, and City Missions are also Christian organizations although not linked to any particular church.

SPECIAL GUEST

Why? To hear from someone from a local church and be able to question them.

Invite along a member of a local church to tell how their church meets needs among its members and in their community.

Allow children to ask questions.

 ## Close the pack

The church is God's representative in its neighbourhood.
The Bible tells Christians to love God and love others.

> **Pose the questions:**
> *How does the church show its love for God?* (Worship and obedience)
> *How does the church show its love for others?* (Caring for them)

29

Easter – Seeing wha

Main idea

Jesus was nailed to a cross and died so that we could live forever as God's friends.

Questions answered
by this program

- What's Easter got to do with religion?
- Why did Jesus let them kill him?
- What does it mean: 'Jesus died for us'?

Bible Base

Mark 14:43- 15:39

For the leader

Think about what the children in your group already know about Jesus and Easter and how they have responded to that knowledge. Try to take them one step further in both knowledge and response. Rather than trying to tear down secular ideas of Easter, like rabbits and Easter eggs, many Christians have found it helpful to 'reclaim Easter', that is accept those secular things as a part of the way society celebrates Easter, but also to help others appreciate the deeper meaning of the new life which Jesus' gives.

We suggest you use the CEV phrase 'nailed to the cross' rather than the technical term 'crucify'.

The children will make a paper folding to recall the story of Jesus' death. Little ones will need help to make it work so you might prefer to make one big one and use it to tell the story.

. . . .

 ## Open the pack

EASTER AND US

Why? For the children to express their understandings of Easter so the leader will find out how much they already know.

> *Pose these questions:*
> *When you think about Easter what's the first thing you think of?*
> *What does Easter have to do with us?*
> *What does Easter have to do with Jesus?*

Comment: Easter is the time Christians celebrate when Jesus died and was brought back to life for us.

Dig in

CROSS STORY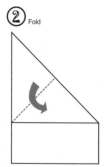

Why? To help children recall what they already know about the cross.

Needed: *1 coloured sheet of A4 paper and a white sheet half the size for each child, scissors, glue*

Using the white (smaller) paper, follow the paper folding diagrams opposite with everyone taking care to keep their own paper pieces Once the foldings have been cut and all the pieces opened out, explain that the pieces help tell part of the Easter story. Ask volunteers to guess what each piece represents and how it fits into the story of Jesus' death. Paste the piece onto the coloured paper in the positions shown in the diagram and read the appropriate Bible passage listed right.

① Fold A4 sheet
② Fold
③ Fold
④ Cut into thirds

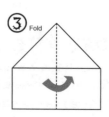
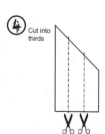

†'s all about

1. Cross Mark 15:1-15
2. Nails Mark 15:24-25
3. Sign on the top of the cross Mark 15:26
4. Two others who died beside Jesus Mark 15:27 – 28
5. Passer by pointing Mark 15:29-32
6. Friends watching Mark 15: 40-41

 ## Chew on it

THE MEANING OF THE CROSS

Why? To get beyond the physical to what happened in the spiritual world when Jesus died.

Needed: Bibles

Comment: We've read the things people saw 2000 years ago when Jesus was nailed to the cross but the Bible says there's a much deeper meaning. Some unique things happened when Jesus died.

Form small groups and challenge the children to read Mark 15:33-39 and find three strange things that happened. *(It was dark for 3 hours in the middle of the day; the curtain in the temple split in two and the army officer was convinced that Jesus was the Son of God.)*

The Bible says these things happened because when Jesus died, in some mysterious way he was dying to take the punishment for our sin. We have all sinned. 'Sin' is when we go against God and do wrong. Sin stops us being friends with God. It was because of our sin that God deserted Jesus on the cross. Jesus died for us.

 ## Close the pack

Ask children to hold their 'cross' picture and imagine Jesus on it. Then imagine all the wrong things they've done nailed to the cross with Jesus.

Comment: Jesus died so we could have a fresh start. If you've never thanked Jesus for dying for you and asked him to take away all the bad things about you, you can do that by saying a 'Thank you , Sorry, Please' prayer.

- **Thank** Jesus for dying on the cross for you
- Say **Sorry** for all the bad things you've done
- Ask Jesus to **Please** forgive you for the times you've let him down and give you a fresh start as his friend.

Anyone who wants to turn away from wrong and be Jesus' friend can pray a prayer like that at any time. You might like to do it this Easter and come back and tell me.

30

Main idea

God brought Jesus back to life and he is alive forever.

Questions answered

by this program

- How did Jesus come alive again when he was dead?
- Why do people think Jesus is so great if he was killed?

Bible Base

Luke 24:1-35

Easter – The Greates

For the leader

It can be helpful for children to realise that even Jesus' disciples were reluctant to believe he had come alive.

The drama will have the most impact if you can get a few competent children to practice it with you beforehand.

When Cleopas and his friend ran to tell the disciples that Jesus was alive again, the disciples already knew because Jesus had appeared to Peter. That appearance is not recorded anywhere in Scripture although it's mentioned again in 1 Corinthians 15:5.

. . . .

 Open the pack

WINNERS

Why? To have some fun introducing the theme of winners.

Needed: *Materials for games*

Run several quick fun activities and find a 'winner' for each. For example:

- Tossing a coin into a polystyrene cup from an increasing distance
- Drawing the best elephant with your eyes closed
- Finding a particular verse in a Bible
- Singing the highest note

Comment: Different people are good at different things. Everyone is a winner at something, but Jesus is the greatest winner of all time.

> **Pose the question:**
> *Why might Jesus' enemies have thought they had won over Jesus?*
> (They had him killed and thought that was the end of him)

 Dig in

ON THE ROAD TO EMMAUS

Why? To tell a Bible story which took place after Jesus was brought back to life.

Needed: *Three copies of Appendix 16, the script*
On the road to Emmaus, *A sign 'Jesus is really alive!'*

Present the drama. *(See For the leader)* Tell the spectators that they have the most important line and that you will hold up a sign to tell them what to say at the right time. Don't let them see the sign beforehand.

> **Pose the question:**
> *How did they know Jesus was really alive?*

Direct the group to Luke 24: 33-34 to find out. *(Jesus had already appeared to Peter.)*

Winner of all Time

Chew on it

THE MOST IMPORTANT PART

Pose the question:
What's so important about Jesus coming back from death?

Bring out these points

1. God brought Jesus alive again because he is really God and had done nothing bad.

2. He's alive, so he can be our friend.

BEFORE AND AFTER PUPPETS

Why? To help process the change that Jesus' friends experienced when they realised he was alive again.

Needed: two circles of card about 10 cm in diameter and a paddle-pop stick for each child. Felt pens. Paper, scissors.

On one circle make a sad face to represent the way Jesus' friends felt when he died and they thought they'd never see him again. On the other circle draw a smiley face to represent the way they felt when they realised Jesus was alive. Tape them together with a paddlepop stick between the circles and some fringed paper for hair.

You could have interviews and ask the puppets why they felt sad and why their feelings changed.

Close the pack

Nothing and no one is more powerful than Jesus. Bad people thought they finished him off but God showed that Jesus is the greatest winner of all time when he brought him back to life. Jesus is alive forever and that makes him the best friend we can ever have.

If you have extra time

EXPLORE

After the drama form groups of 3-6 and have each group explore one of the narratives about Jesus coming back to life in these passages:

Matthew 28: 1-7, Matthew 28: 8-15, Mark 16:1-8, Mark 16: 9-14, Luke 24: 36-43, Luke 24:1-11, John 20: 1-10, John 20:1-18, John 20: 19- 29, John 21:1-14

Let the groups share what they discovered.

ALIVE POSTERS

Make posters together announcing that Jesus is alive forever.

Christmas - The Rea

Main idea

Christmas is a time to celebrate the birth of Jesus.

Questions

answered

by this program

- What's the point of Christmas?
- How can I find out what Christmas is really about?
- What has an animal feed box and shepherds got to do with Christmas?

Bible Base

Matthew 1: 18- 2: 16, Luke 2: 1-19

For the leader

Think of the different images of Christmas which confront children. Where if anywhere, do they encounter the voice of God announcing the birth of his child, born to die for the world?

Before you begin, read the accounts of Jesus' birth in Matthew and Luke. Note the ordinariness of the location, the status of the people involved, the wonder of the announcement, the earthiness of the birth, the reactions of the visitors. This birth was, and is today, an enigma. Why did God choose Bethlehem, an insignificant virgin, shepherds and scholars from a distant land? Take time to reflect on the wonders of the whole event and spend time listening to the still small voice of God. Chapter 2 of Phillip Yancey's book *The Jesus I Never Knew* (Zondervan) gives fresh insights into Jesus' birth.

. . . .

 Open the pack

CHINESE WHISPERS

Why? An illustration of the meaning of Christmas being messed up.

Comment: This is like Christmas. Over the years the real message of Christmas has got jumbled up and confused. It's hard to know what Christmas is really about anymore but the real meaning is amazing.

JUNK MAIL MAYHEM

Why? To acknowledge that to many people Christmas is about presents.

Needed: *Multiple copies of various Christmas shopping catalogues*

Prepare a brief quiz with questions from each catalogue. Give each team a set of catalogues. Call out each question. The first team to find the answer and reach you with it gains a point.

Comment: There are lots of confusing messages around about Christmas. To some people it's all about buying and selling, but the real meaning of Christmas is amazing.

 Dig in

THE FIRST CHRISTMAS

Why? To get the real story from the Bible.

Needed: *Bibles*

Comment: The Bible gives an account of the first Christmas.

Divide the children into groups and allocate a character from the Christmas story to each group. Give each group the relevant passages below to read. Challenge them to find as many facts as they can about the events concerning their character in the Christmas story.

Story

- Mary: Matthew 1:18-24 Luke 1:26-38; 2:5-7
- Joseph: Matthew 1:18-24; 2:13-15, 19-23 Luke 2:1-7
- Herod: Matthew 2:1-12, 16
- Shepherds: Luke 2:8-20
- Wise Men: Matthew 2:1-12

Reassemble the children and ask a couple of questions to each group, choosing different children. Your questioning, and the children's answers, will reveal the events of this occasion as seen through the eyes of the people involved.

HERE'S THE STORY

Needed: A video or picture story book about Christmas.

Show a video or read a picture book of the Christmas story. Choose one that keeps to the facts and doesn't over sentimentalise Christ's birth. Alternatively read the accounts from Matthew and Luke, asking the children to watch out for three things they didn't know before.

Chew on it

WHAT DO YOU THINK?

Why? To help process the Bible story.

> *Pose the questions:*
> *Now you've read the original account of the first Christmas, what do you think is most amazing about it? Why?*

Invite leaders and children to answer. You might cover things like God coming to earth in human form, Jesus' birth being predicted in the Bible and ordinary people being involved.

TREE ACTIVITY

Why? To emphasis the fact that Jesus came for each of us.

Needed: Christmas tree, star shaped cardboard shapes, hole punch, ribbon, glitter glue, felt pens

Give each child a star shape cut out of coloured card with a loop of string threaded through the top. The children write their names on their star and decorate with tinsel or glitter before hanging it on the tree.

Comment: God knows each of us by name and we are very important to him. That's why he sent Jesus into this world so we could live as his friends forever. Christmas is for celebrating Jesus' coming.

Close the pack

Talk together briefly about what would make God send his son from heaven to a dirty, stable in a remote little town. It shows God's great love for each of us.

Invite the children to silently tell God how it makes them feel to be loved so much. Encourage them to be honest with God.

Finish by praying that you will all celebrate the real meaning of Christmas this year.

Main idea

Jesus came to show God's love to the world.

Questions

answered

by this program

- How was Jesus' birth different to mine?
- What do the events surrounding Jesus' birth tell me about him?

Bible Base

Matthew 1:18-25, Luke 2:1-20

Christmas – The Why

For the leader

Sadly our Christmas carols, cards and literature often paint an unreal picture of Jesus' birth. We have 'the little Lord Jesus, no crying he makes', nativity scenes full of cute angels and halos and storybooks full of sterile stables and pet-like animals.

The facts we read in the Gospel accounts are very different. We read of an inexperienced teenager and her husband in a strange town, forced to sleep in a makeshift bed of hay. It is here, that Jesus is born and laid in the animals' feeding trough. How many mothers today would be prepared to put their newborn in such a place?

Read Matthew 1: 18-25 and Luke 2:1-20, as if reading it for the first time. We're actually told very little about Jesus' birth. It is a stark picture in comparison to that in today's storybooks and songs.

Now read John 1:1-13. John doesn't even describe the scene of Jesus' birth. He simply announces it. For John the important thing was to tell us *why* he came.

In this session, try to use the facts of the birth to point to the reason for the birth.

· ·

  Open the pack

BABY TIME

Why? To focus on birth.

Needed: A willing mother and baby

Invite a friend to bring in her baby and interview her to find out such things as when and where the baby was born, who came to visit and what presents were given. If possible let some children hold the baby. Invite children to share what they remember about when little brothers and sisters were born.

WHO'S THAT?

Why? To emphasis the fact that every person was once born.

Needed: Numbered pictures of celebrities, school staff, club leaders and others known to the children. (They can be baby photos but any photos will do.) Pencils and paper.

Display the pictures and ask the children to write the numbers and who they think each person is. Mark the quiz together and have a small prize for the winner!

Comment: People are so different but one thing we all have in common is that we were born! Jesus was born too, but he was a very different baby.

 # Dig in

MARY'S STORY

Why? To review the unusual events surrounding Jesus' birth.

Needed: *Two copies of Appendix 17* Mary and Elizabeth chat.

Have two leaders present the play.

Talk together about things that were different about Jesus' birth compared to an average birth today.

> **Pose the question:**
> *What do you think the things that were different about Jesus' birth tell us about him?*

A DIFFERENT BIRTH

Needed: *Board or other materials to make a list.*

On the board head up two columns 'Jesus' Birth' and 'My Birth'.

Children follow in their Bibles as you, or a volunteer, reads Luke 2:1-20. Stop after each verse to see if a fact about the birth of Jesus can be added to the board such as 'laid on a bed of hay' or 'dressed in baby clothes'. (Choose different children to list these in turn on the board).

After each fact is added to the 'Jesus' Birth' side, ask, 'Was this the same for your birth?' Choose a different child each time to add the modern day equivalent such as 'put in a hospital crib'. Most will be different but there may be one or two similarities such as 'dressed in baby clothes' (although regular baby clothes in those days were strips of cloth rather than all-in-one suits.)

 # Chew on it

WHAT DOES IT MEAN?

Why? To follow up the *A Different Birth* activity above.

In small groups or all together, decide which was the most different or unusual aspect of Jesus' birth and what it might tell us about Jesus.

PEOPLE CHAINS

Needed: *At least five strips of Christmas paper about 2cm x 15 cm for each child, glue, marker pens.*

Invite the children to write the names of people who are special to them as well as their own names on the paper strips then make up the paper chain using glue. Hang the chain around the room.

Comment: God loves each of these people so much that he was prepared to send his own son, Jesus, to earth so that each person here could be his friend.

Volunteers could pray a prayer of thanks for Jesus or pray that each person named on the chain would respond to God and become God's friend.

 # Close the pack

Needed: Gospelling to the Beat 1 *CD and CD player.*

Display the words and play the song *Jesus came* which tells why Jesus came to earth.
Invite the group to sing along.

See how many of these "G'day" activities you can complete. Every time you meet someone say "G'day", introduce yourself, do the activity and get them to sign under it

Get someone to join you in singing the theme song to your favourite TV show.

Signature

_____

Ask 3 people who their favourite band is and write them down here ...

_____

_____

Signatures

_____

_____

Find 2 people with the same size shoe as you.

Signatures

_____

_____

Feed a new friend a biscuit (get it from a leader)

Signature

_____

Sit on the floor facing another person. Hold hands, put the soles of your feet together and stand up!

Signature

_____

Say

Stand back to back with someone and tell each other what sports you like.

Signature

_____

Do 5 pushups with someone from a different year to you and find out who their teacher is!

Signature

_____

Find a leader, say "Hi" and see what happens! (Only once for each leader!)

Find a new friend and together find 5 words with 3 or more letters in "SUPA WELCOMES YOU".

Write them here.

_____
_____
_____
_____
_____

Find someone who forgot to brush their teeth this morning!

"G'day"!

The inhabitants of Ig

The inhabitants of Og

HOW to TURN to GOD

Jesus died on the cross so we can be forgiven for choosing sin instead of God's way.

Jesus made a way to take away our sin so we can be friends with God.

BACK ON TRACK

Sin stops us from being friends with God. Although God welcomes us, sin gets in the way.

When we don't do what God wants, the Bible calls it sin.

WRONG WAY GO BACK

All of us have made choices that take us away from God rather than closer to him.

We all make choices every day. Sometimes we choose what's right and good, but not always.

Please
Ask God to live in your life and give you a new start. Ask for God's help to keep turning away from sin.

Sorry
Tell God you are sorry for the sin in your life. Ask God to forgive you.

Thank you
Say thanks to God for loving you and for making a way for you to be forgiven and come back to God. Thank Jesus for showing us the way to live and for dying for us.

If you want to turn away from sin and *towards* God, you need to pray a 'thank you – sorry-please' prayer. It goes like this ...

Stories Jesus Told

The Sower

The Lost Sheep

The Good Samaritan

Hidden Treasure

Letters from Disciples to

Timothy

The Church at Rome

All Christians

The Church at Phillippi

Wise Sayings About

Living God's Way

What Life's About

Stories About Jesus

His Birth

Feeding 5 Thousand

Going to Heaven

The Storm

Dying on the Cross

Songs About

Great Escapes

God's Love

Jesus' Birth

Loving God

Praising God

Messages from God to

Isaiah

John

Jeremiah

Jonah

What's in the Bible

Stories About God's People

Esther

Nehemiah

Paul

Tabitha

Peter

JAFFA

THE BIBLE is the story of God and his people

THE BIBLE is the story of God and his people

THE BIBLE is the story of God and his people

THE BIBLE is the story of God and his people

THE BIBLE is the story of God and his people

THE BIBLE is the story of God and his people

Cut into separate questions.   One set for each team of 3-6.

1 Exodus 9:22-28
In what country did this storm happen?

2 Luke 8:22-25
What was Jesus doing during this storm?

3 Acts 27:13-20
What did the sailors wrap around the ship to stop it falling apart in this storm?

1 Exodus 9:22-28
In what country did this storm happen?

2 Luke 8:22-25
What was Jesus doing during this storm?

3 Acts 27:13-20
What did the sailors wrap around the ship to stop it falling apart in this storm?

1 Exodus 9:22-28
In what country did this storm happen?

2 Luke 8:22-25
What was Jesus doing during this storm?

3 Acts 27:13-20
What did the sailors wrap around the ship to stop it falling apart in this storm?

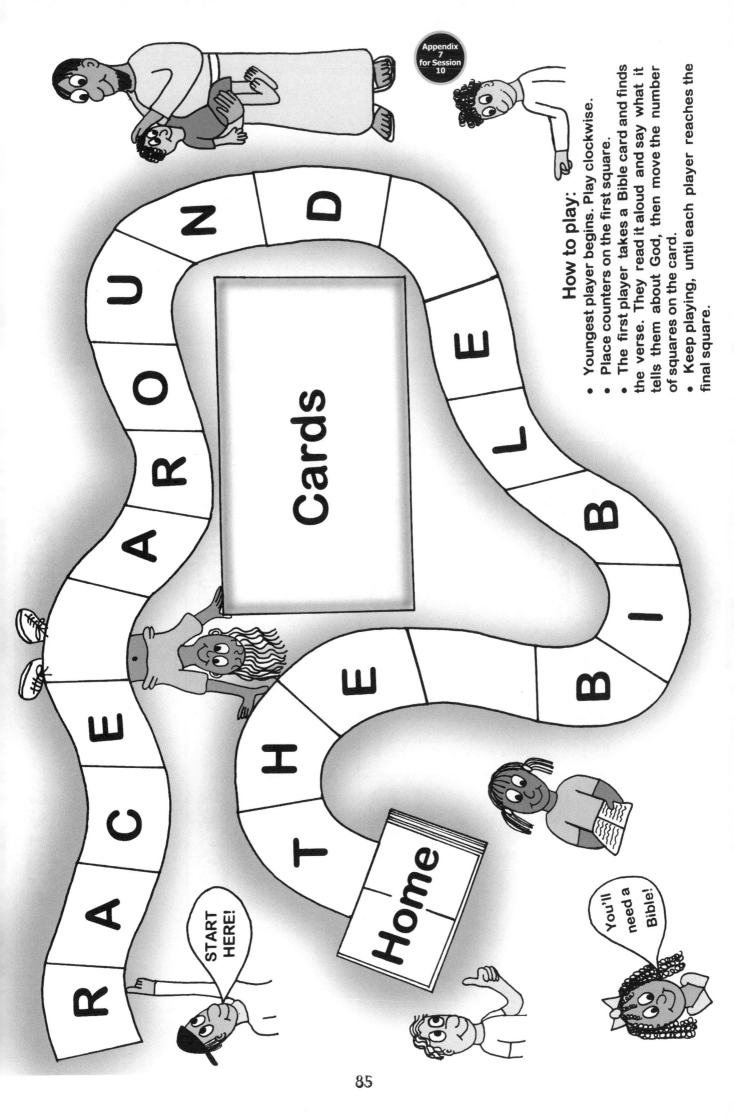

Race Around the Bible Game Cards for Session 10 *(See board previous page)*

Prepare 60 of the cards below with the following Bible references. Place the pile onto the board game. The number of moves forward are indicated on each card.

Psalm 27:1	Psalm 111:7	Psalm 34:8	Joshua 3:5
Genesis 1:1	James 1:17	Romans 11:36	Jude 24-25
Psalm 23:1	Mark 4:39	1 Corinthians 1:25	Numbers 23:19
Psalm 86:8	Proverbs 15:3	Job 33:6b	1 Kings 8:56
Acts 17:24	Joshua 1:9	Malachi 3:6	Jeremiah 51:15
Philippians 4:13	Isaiah 41:10	Colossians 1:16	2 Peter 3:13
1 Chronicles 29:11	Matthew 10:29-30	1 Peter 1:25	Psalm 139:13
Isaiah 40:11	Romans 8:38	Hebrews 13:8	Deuteronomy 29:29
Colossians 3:12	1 John 3:1	2 Corinthians 9:8	Hebrews 13:5
Jeremiah 31:3	1 John 4:9	Ephesians 2:10	
1 John 4:19	John 3:16	Romans 3:21	

MOVE 1	MOVE 2	MOVE 3	MOVE 4

MOVE 1	MOVE 2	MOVE 3	MOVE 4

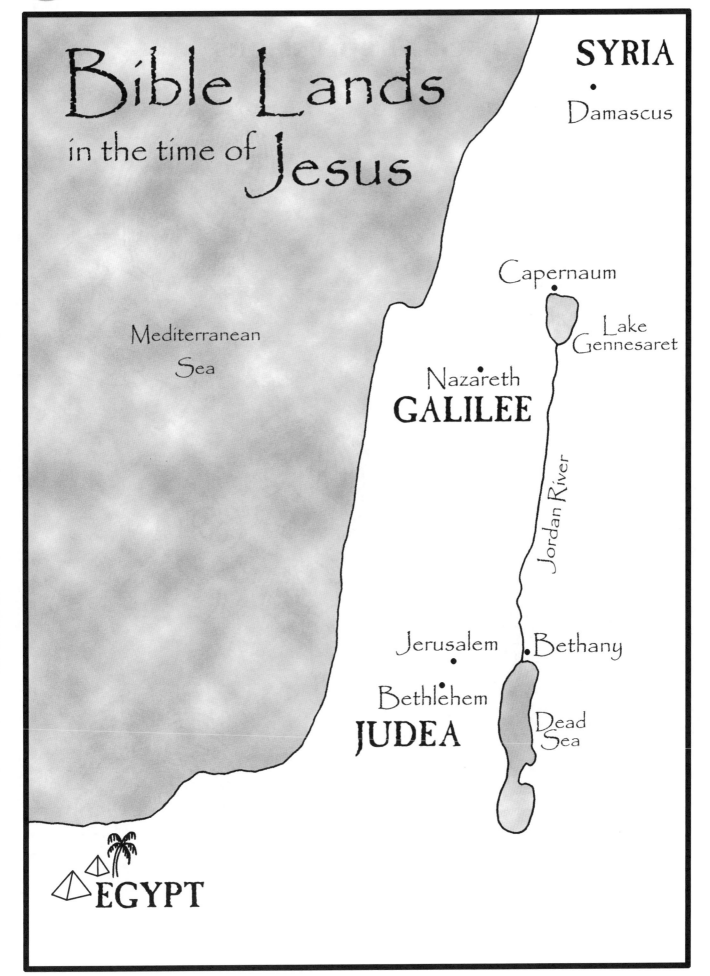

Facial Expressions

Thankyou for the invitation to the party in Heaven

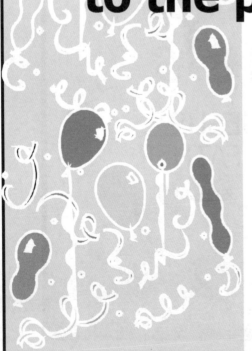

◯ I decided to be part of the celebrations some time ago. I will be there.

◯ I would like to come but need more help to know how to get there.

◯ I need to think more about it before I decide.

◯ It sounds great but I would like to know more about following Jesus.

Thankyou for the invitation to the party in Heaven

◯ I decided to be part of the celebrations some time ago. I will be there.

◯ I would like to come but need more help to know how to get there.

◯ I need to think more about it before I decide.

◯ It sounds great but I would like to know more about following Jesus.

Situation cards

Someone tells you they know
something nasty about a
friend of yours.

What do you do?

A friend tells you that you
look awful in some new
clothes you've just bought.

What do you do?

A friend tells you that another
friend has been saying nasty
things about you.

What do you do?

Some friends want you to
help them graffiti the fences
in the street next to yours.

What do you do?

A friend wants you
to tell his parents he was
at your house after school,
even though he wasn't.

What do you do?

A friend tells you that they
stole some chocolate bars
from the local shop?

What do you do?

Ask questions of the other person and yourself

◯ Is it wrong?

◯ Will I be upset or hurt?

◯ Will I be sorry afterwards?

◯ Will it disappoint my family?

Say 'NO' if the answer to any of these questions is 'yes'

Know positive options

◯ Suggest something else

◯ If the person doesn't accept, leave.

Ask questions of the other person and yourself

◯ Is it wrong?

◯ Will I be upset or hurt?

◯ Will I be sorry afterwards?

◯ Will it disappoint my family?

Say 'NO' if the answer to any of these questions is 'yes'

Know positive options

◯ Suggest something else

◯ If the person doesn't accept, leave.

Samuel and Eli script

Narrator 1: This is the story of a priest in God's temple …

Eli: That's me. My name is Eli.

Narrator 1: …and a little boy …

Samuel: That's me. My name is Samuel.

Narrator 1: …who was learning to be a priest. In those days God hardly ever communicated directly with people and he didn't appear to them in dreams very often. One night, Eli …

Eli: That's me.

Narrator 1: …was asleep in his room in the temple and Samuel …

Samuel: That's me, the little boy who was learning to be a priest.

Narrator 1: …was sleeping on a mat near the sacred chest in the temple. They hadn't been asleep for long when God called out Samuel's name.

Voice: Samuel. Samuel.

Narrator 1: Samuel jumped out of bed. He ran to Eli's room.

Samuel: That's right. I said 'Here I am Eli. What do you want?'

Eli: And I said, 'I didn't call you. Go back to bed.'

Narrator 1: So Samuel went back to bed.

Samuel: I did. But it wasn't long before I heard the voice again.

Voice: Samuel, Samuel.

Narrator 1: Samuel jumped up and ran to the old priest again. He said …

Samuel: Here I am. What do you want?

Eli: And I said, 'I didn't call you. Go back to bed.'

Narrator 2: How many times does his go on?

Narrator 1: It happened one more time. Then Eli realised what was happening. He told Samuel to go back to bed and lie down and be ready to listen when it happened again.

Narrator 2: And did it?

Narrator 1: God came to Samuel and called his name again.

Samuel: And I said, 'I'm listening, God. What do you want me to do?'

Narrator 1: God talked to Samuel and told him what he was going to do and Samuel passed on God's message to the priest.

Narrator 2: I've got a question. Where did you hear this story?

Narrator 1: In the Bible.

Narrator 2: Is that the end?

Narrator 1: It is for now .But it wasn't for Samuel. It was just the start of Samuel's amazing life of being God's messenger.

Narrator 2: Can I take a bow then?

Narrator 1: I think we should all take a bow while everyone else claps.

On the Road to Emmaus

Characters:	Narrator, Cleopas, his friend, Jesus. **The rest of the group will be the disciples back in Jerusalem and will shout together 'Hey Jesus is really alive!' at the end.**
Narrator:	It is the Sunday after Jesus was nailed to the cross. Two of Jesus followers were on their way to a village called Emmaus. It was 11 kilometres and they had to walk. The two unhappy disciples were talking to each other about all the things that had happened.
Cleopas:	I'm glad that horrible weekend is over. It was so senseless.
Friend:	I really thought Jesus was the Son of God. But he can't be. He's dead.
Cleopas:	We all thought that. But he's been buried for three days.
Narrator:	With the glare of the setting sun in front of them, and with so many sad things to say to each other, they did not take much notice of the third traveller who caught up with them.
Jesus:	How come you guys are so sad?
Cleopas:	You must be the only person around here who hasn't heard the news.
Jesus:	What news?
Friend:	About Jesus and how they nailed him to a cross. Jesus is dead.
Cleopas:	We thought God had sent him to be our new king, the one we Jews had been waiting for.
Friend:	But three days ago the Romans killed him.
Cleopas:	And then we hear that now the body has gone missing. It's all so confusing.
Friend:	Some people say angels have said he's alive. None of this makes any sense.
Narrator:	As they continued their homeward journey they didn't seem to notice the smile growing on the stranger's face.
Jesus:	Your trouble is that you don't know your Scriptures. Can't you see? God told you his Son would have to die. It's all there. Give me the Scriptures and let me explain.
Narrator:	By the time they reached Emmaus, they were both feeling strangely excited. The man travelling with them was making sense of the events of the weekend.
Cleopas:	You simply must spend the night with us.
Friend:	Yes! Stay with us! It's getting dark.
Narrator:	The three sat down to their meal. The stranger gave thanks and broke the bread, just like Jesus had done. Suddenly he was gone!
Cleopas:	No wonder we felt so marvellous. How could we have been so stupid and not realised it was Jesus!
Friend:	Quick! Let's go back to Jerusalem and tell the others.
Narrator:	They raced back to the other disciples to tell them the great news. But when they knocked on the door, all the disciples shouted out …
Everyone:	**Jesus is really alive!**

Mary and Elizabeth chat

Mary and Joseph took Jesus to Egypt when he was little because Herod wanted to kill him.
We don't know how long they were there, but after Herod died they returned to Nazareth.
Here's an imaginary meeting of Mary and her cousin Elizabeth.

Mary (calling out): Elizabeth, are you there?

Elizabeth: Mary, it's so good to see you again after so long and so much has happened since we last met. And this is Jesus! What a beautiful child!

Mary: It's wonderful to see you too. I haven't had much of a chance to talk to other women about what has happened so I'm looking forward to a long chat.

Elizabeth: Come on inside and take the weight of your feet, would you like something to drink?

Mary: Oh, yes please, it's a long way from Nazareth and we're really very tired.

Elizabeth: So tell me Mary, what has been happening to you?

Mary: Well you know how Emperor Augustus called a census just as Jesus was due to be born and everyone had to go back to the town they were born. Joseph's from Bethlehem, so we headed for there. I can tell you it was a really difficult time with the baby so big and such a long way to walk.

Elizabeth: You poor darling, you could have had the baby out there in the middle of nowhere!

Mary: Yes, but God was caring for us both, it was a really amazing time for us. When we got to Bethlehem all the rooms were taken and all we could find was a stable out the back of an inn. That's where Jesus was born. We had to use the animals feeding trough and straw to lay him in. Then a group of shepherds arrived. They had been watching their sheep and suddenly an angel appeared to them.

Elizabeth: Just like one came to Zechariah and you?

Mary: Yes! The angel told them to go to Bethlehem and there they would find a baby in a feed trough. The angel said the baby was the Saviour of the world. You can imagine how we felt when they turned up!

Elizabeth: I don't suppose you were really ready for visitors. What did they do?

Mary: They sat in the hay and told us their story. Apparently they saw lots of angels and everything was dazzling bright. They were laughing and couldn't get over the fact that Jesus was lying there in the feed trough, just like the angel had told them. Other people came and listened to what they had to say. And then they went back to their sheep.

Elizabeth: What a night!

Mary: That's not all! We settled in Bethlehem for a while. Then when Jesus was a toddler these Kings or Wise Men from an Eastern Country appeared on our doorstep. They had been following a very special star for ages and it had led them right to our front door!

Elizabeth: My goodness, what did you do?

Mary: I honestly didn't know what I should do. But they seemed to take matters into their own hands and invited themselves in to see Jesus who they said was the Messiah, sent from God. They gave him some very expensive gifts. They even bowed down to worship him. And they were kings!

Elizabeth: So Mary what do you make of all this?

Mary: I'm really not sure. Every day I think about all the things that have happened. I guess I'm just going to have to trust God to show Joseph and I how to bring up this very special child. The angel told me when he visited me before I became pregnant that this child would be called the Son of God and would save his people and be their King. I guess I just praise God for choosing me, and do my best.

Elizabeth: It's all so amazing. You're right. You need to praise and trust God. I do too.
We could go and spend some time praising God now. Will you come with me?

Mary: Yes, I'd love to! (Both women exit)

These are the resources our children's ministry coordinators voted the most useful. All are available from your nearest Scripture Union Resource Centre and most Christian bookshops.

Bibles & Bible Reading

The Bible Society's **Contemporary English Version of the Bible** is in simple English and is suitable for all ages. It's the one most recommended for use with children.

Hotshots

Eight books in the series, designed for children to enjoy Bible reading, puzzles, stories and faith building activities.

Safety & Care

Safety and Care manual covers the main issues of safety and care of children in programs, recruitment of leaders, codes of practice.

Music

Gospelling to the Beat 1 and **2** each contain fifty songs for use in outreach with children. A thematic index and teaching tips are useful additions. Music books and CDs of each are available.

TALKING WITH CHILDREN ABOUT FOLLOWING JESUS

Starting Out

... is an excellent tool to use with 7-11's to help them understand how to take their first steps in responding to Jesus and following him.

5 Things God Wants Me to Know/Do

... is a useful leaflet designed for leaders to use with 5-8 year olds who want to know more about following Jesus.

Join the Team

... is an 8 session program to help 10-12's understand the message of salvation. It has Bible activities, games, song suggestions and take home Team Challenge sheets to help interested kids work out what the cross has to do with them.

GAMES

Theme Games

... by Lesley Pinchbeck has around 150 games arranged thematically and well indexed so you can easily find a time stretcher to fit your program.

CRAFT

Here's One I Made Earlier and Here's Another One I Made Earlier

... are two books of tried and tested craft ideas for 3-11 year olds.

LEADER TRAINING

Come and Follow

... by Cecily Cupit is a helpful resource for leaders packed with information and practical tips on how to point children to Jesus in ways suitable to their age and background.

Keeping In Touch

... is a quarterly magazine for adults who work with children in the upper grades of primary school. It contains feature articles on contemporary issues, resource and website reviews, program ideas, photocopiable ideas and much more. Subscriptions available from SU offices.